Additional Credit:

Cover design - POPSymbol.com

Research - Publishing Services

Writing - Norah Jackson

Editing - Marilyn Bell

Visit the blog at KyrabeStories.com for more helpful resources.

Complete the Series

Grab a copy of *She's Meant to Lead* and *She's Meant to Speak* to complement what you are about to learn within *She's Meant to Negotiate*! The collection can be read in any order that you see fit for your goals.

Scan for Book
Collection

Contents

Introduction

"A strong woman understands that the gifts such as logic, decisiveness, and strength are just as feminine as intuition and emotional connection. She values and uses all of her gifts."
Nancy Rathburn

Let me begin by telling you a story that—in a rather circuitous manner—led to the creation of this negotiation book. Back in 2018, I held a sales position in an organization. While there were some good things about the organization—and many of their pitches made sense—most of their sales tactics didn't appeal to my introverted nature. I found them rather aggressive and even disrespectful to the customers in some cases. Even though I made good sales on some days, their strategies took a massive toll on my mental well-being. So much so that one day, I had a social anxiety breakdown and ended up hyperventilating in the middle of my shift, terrifying my poor coworker in the process. That is when I knew I wasn't cut out for this job and decided that day to quit.

This short phase in my life left me with lessons for a lifetime. I learned firsthand how important it was for me to identify what made me feel unsupported or uncomfortable in a work environment. I also understood the need to advocate for myself in a professional setting and to draw clear boundaries regarding my work and my interactions with others. I found it challenging to speak up in social and professional settings, especially if I was new to the space, but this experience taught me that no one else could do this for me.

I began to see sales in a different light and learned, perhaps for the first time, how negotiation is less about getting the other party to accept your demands and more about creating win-win solutions for both parties. I also learned that, whether we like it or not, we're almost always "selling" ourselves to another person—be it for personal or professional reasons. Therefore, it helps to know what makes us valuable to other people. An essential lesson for me was that sales or negotiation isn't about lying or exaggerating; it's about making sure that the other party knows our worth and treats us accordingly. Most importantly, I discovered that many of the qualities that I saw as weaknesses were actually strengths when it came to negotiating.

Upon combining the tactics I did agree with in my sales stint with my own strengths, I decided to create something of my own. I delved deep into the concepts of psychology and marketing that would allow me to connect with people in a meaningful way. These connections could then become the foundation for the development of products and services that could enhance their lives.

That rather scary wake-up call led to the creation of the *Kyrabe Stories* blog in 2019. The blog was launched with the aim of helping people with their professional development against the background of an ever-changing workplace. This blog led to exciting collaborations with LinkedIn Learning and the Wall Street Journal, which in turn helped me pitch myself more and land a marketing specialist position at an e-learning company. Not only was this a higher-paying position, but it also aligned more with my empathetic core values. The organization truly cared about connecting with its customers, and I felt exceptionally lucky to have a supervisor who appreciated my strengths, identified my potential improvement areas, and took the initiative to guide me and help me channel my skills to increase the customer base in an ethical and considerate manner.

One good thing led to another, and the knowledge and student engagement I gained in that organization helped me connect and collaborate with other skilled individuals to successfully publish these books, with the biggest achievement being inspiring women all over the country with the "She's Meant to Be" series. None of this would have been possible if I hadn't found my voice to negotiate for something more, something better than what was available to me at the time.

I'm telling you this story because all of this started with a heartbreak and a sobering realization. If you feel like you're at the end of your tether, I want you to know that this is only the beginning. If you feel lost today, it only means that you get to determine your path from now on.

As women, we're frequently made aware of the unique challenges we face when we try to negotiate for ourselves, and I've also seen what happens when we stay the course and keep fighting for our voices to be heard. This book was born out of the fact that women are meant to negotiate, even if it gets tough at times, and even if the world seems to be telling us not to bother.

If you're someone who doubts whether you are a good negotiator or not, here's a direct signal for you: When women negotiate on someone else's behalf, they usually perform better than men (Dalla-Camina, 2023). This clearly shows that women don't lack negotiation skills, nor are they poor negotiators "by nature." Why, then, do women fare poorly when it comes to negotiating for themselves? The answer is a combination of factors. One, women still have to bear the brunt of stereotypes against them. For example, people are more likely to lie when a woman is negotiating with them. One of the reasons for this is that they see women as less competent than men and, hence, less likely to figure out their lies.

More importantly, women have to face a tough choice when it comes to negotiating for themselves. On one hand, many women are conditioned to believe that they are not good enough to ask for raises, promotions, or even projects they like. As such, women usually don't ask for something unless they are told it is okay to do so. Men, however, negotiate all the time—even for things they might not really be qualified for. On the other hand, when women start negotiating for themselves, they are seen as aggressive and unlikeable—not only by men but also by women (Shonk, 2024e). Therefore, even if a woman believes in her own capabilities, she is likely aware that negotiating can make things tougher for her than it would for a man.

Does this mean that we give up, that there's no hope for us? Not at all. If anything, we need to double down and start seeing things from a different, more empowered perspective. There are a few aspects of the negotiation journey that we will focus on in this book. First, we will discuss ways to recognize our true worth. Then, we'll talk about the various challenges that women face while negotiating, after which we will move on to different strategies we can use to negotiate effectively for ourselves. This book also aims to widen the scope of what negotiation can do—for example, we will talk about negotiating for more than a higher salary—and to help us avoid some of the common pitfalls on our negotiating journey.

This book isn't about unbridled or unrealistic optimism. It understands that the playing field is not even for men and women when it comes to negotiation, but it also refuses to give in to the narrative of despondence that surrounds it. If you're someone who is just starting their negotiation journey, or if you've faced certain rejections along the way, it might be difficult to be hopeful about the future. The thing is, most—if not all—of the rights that women enjoy today have been granted to us because women in the past advocated for themselves and fought for a place at the table. This book hopes to encourage you to keep going and keep learning on your own journey—not just for yourself but to also make it easier for the women around and after you.

Ultimately, this is a book about challenging our own as well as others' imaginations about what women can do when they believe in themselves. No matter the gender, no one can help us if we refuse to help ourselves first. Remember, your reality could help revitalize someone else's imagination, and there's no bigger gift that we can give each other in a world that constantly tests our faith and patience.

PART 1:
RECOGNIZE YOUR WORTH

1

Embracing Your Worth—The Foundation of Successful Negotiation

*"The most important relationship in your life is the relationship you have with
yourself."*
Diane Von Furstenberg

This world often presents a strange conundrum to us. On one hand, no one can determine our inherent worth. In fact, our self-worth doesn't depend on external markers of success. On the other hand, if we want to advocate for ourselves in various situations, we need to be able to communicate our worth to others. Think of it this way: If we cannot tell someone what we are worth, they're going to assume our value and treat us accordingly. If we're extremely lucky, they might overvalue us, but we all know how rare that is. Chances are, we are going to be overlooked, devalued, and essentially taken for granted in most of our interactions with others. To negotiate successfully, we should mainly focus on two things. First, we need to recognize and embrace our worth, and second, we need to communicate it effectively to others. In this chapter, we will focus on recognizing our worth and learning to communicate it in an assertive manner. Let's begin by embracing our "unique value proposition."

Understanding Your Unique Value Proposition

Before you advocate for yourself in professional settings, it's important to determine what you bring to the table. Your "unique value proposition" is the sum of your skills, experience, and achievements—things that differentiate you from others and that can add value to a team or an organization.

Conducting a Personal Skills Inventory

In a fast-changing world, it has become even more important to learn and relearn various skills that keep us relevant and in demand. While some of these skills are technical in nature and specific to the industry we currently work in, most of them are transferrable and industry-agnostic. When we create a personal skills inventory, we become familiar with the skills we possess, those we don't, and those we need to acquire as urgently as possible. Also, since some skills can become obsolete in this world, we need to keep revisiting our "arsenal" to make sure we are ready for our most relevant professional challenges. Let's create a personal skills inventory for this:

1. Use a notebook or an Excel spreadsheet to create various categories of skills that you need.

2. Start with technical skills that pertain to your industry, then move on to technical skills that can become relevant in the next few years or those that can disrupt your role. For instance, if AI can take over certain aspects of your current role, you'll need to learn how to work with it and upskill yourself accordingly.

3. Move on to broader skills that can be applied in various jobs and

industries. These would include problem-solving skills, creative skills, and number skills.

4. In the last part of this exercise, focus on those soft skills that make you stand out. For example, communication skills, active listening and empathy skills, people management skills, and emotional intelligence skills.

5. Once you've decided which skills are ideal for you to focus on, break them down into actionable points. For instance, communication skills can be broken down into written communication skills—like crafting and responding to emails—and verbal presentation skills. Communication can also include nonverbal skills like gestures, body language, and tone. Start with only two or three subcategories so that you don't get overwhelmed.

6. For each action point, write down whether you're confident about it, whether you could develop it further, or if you're really unsure about it.

7. Based on the current status of your skills, you'll need to decide whether you can include them in your unique value proposition or if you require assistance in developing them.

Reflecting on Your Key Achievements and Impact

One of the most compelling ways to showcase your worth to others is by discussing your achievements and impact in clear terms. A key point to remember while doing this exercise is that not all achievements are quantifiable. If you can show how some of your efforts at your workplace have led to measurable results—for example, if a sales tactic you used led to an increase in sales—that's great. At the same time, it's a good idea to look for qualitative effects of your skills and behaviors on your teammates and others you work with.

One template that can be impactful is outlining the scope of your current or previous roles, detailing the actions you took, and then talking about your achievements. This way, the other party knows how to contextualize your achievements. Here are a few different kinds of achievements you can focus on:

- rewards and recognitions specific to your organization or team

- industry-wide recognitions

- achievements against targets set for the quarter or year

- leadership-specific recognition—for example, if you're in charge of managing a team and their performance has improved under your guidance

- an increase in responsibilities—when it happens after mutual agreement between you and your manager—can also be a great indicator of your professional achievements

- implementation of a new system in your workplace

- mentoring newcomers in the organization

Articulating Your Contributions to the Organization

Once you've understood what you bring to the table, remember to clearly and effectively articulate it to others. There are many reasons why you should spend time crafting a compelling value proposition statement. Think of it this way: When you choose to support a particular brand of product, you're responding—either consciously or otherwise—to their value proposition. You're asking yourself—why should I choose this brand instead of another, or what does this brand give me that no other brand can? When you negotiate for yourself, you are essentially marketing yourself as a brand and telling the other person to choose you over others. Let's discuss the steps needed to craft an effective value proposition statement:

1. Think deeply about your skills and achievements so far. The exercises we've done earlier will help you make a note of them.

2. For each achievement or skill, choose one example that supports it. Suppose if you're claiming to be a creative problem-solver, you need to back it up with a relevant example in the workplace.

3. Pay attention to what makes you unique. Ask yourself the following questions: How does my presence add to a certain scenario? What is it that only I can bring to a situation? If I'm asked to mentor someone in the organization, what could they learn specifically from me—something they might not be able to learn elsewhere?

4. Make a list of the expectations that your seniors or team members might have from you regarding different projects. These expectations are usually in sync with the scope of the project. You can also look at your key performance indicators for the quarter or year to get an idea of what's expected from you. Then, after the specified period is over, take note of whether you've met or exceeded those expectations. Pay attention to instances where you've gone above and beyond your job description to create a meaningful impact in your organization or work.

What a Value Proposition Statement Looks Like

Think of a value proposition statement as the description that convinces the other person to invest in your growth. A simple template to follow while creating your statement is:

- I am _____ (Who are you, what is your job description, and what are one or two adjectives to describe yourself?)

- My offering is _____ (What are the qualities that you bring to the table?)

- My qualities help _____ (Who are you "pitching" to? Who is your target audience?)

- I can help resolve _____ (What is the pain point of your audience, or why do they need you on the team?)

- You can rely on me because _____ (What differentiates you from others who could be negotiating for similar things? What is your "proof of concept?")

In one sentence, the statement can look like this: I am _____ offering _____ to _____ with _____ because _____.

Let's take an example that makes it clearer. Suppose you're negotiating for a consultant role with companies in the creative industry. These are companies that have carved a niche for themselves but are not very big in the space.

Your value proposition statement could look like this: I am a **passionate marketer** (*who am I?*) who has worked as a consultant for many organizations in the creative industry, and I'm offering my services to **mid- and small-scale organizations that are disrupting this space** (*who am I targeting?*). Since the **creative industry can lack organization** (*why might they need me?*), you need an experienced person to help you navigate the challenges you face within it. As someone with **almost 10 years of experience** (*why am I good at this?*) in the industry and who has successfully **helped organizations** like [names of previous organizations you've consulted for] **achieve x% of year-on-year growth** (*proof of concept*), I can be of immense assistance to you. What sets me apart from most of my contemporaries is that I've been **a practitioner in the industry and possess insider knowledge** (*unique selling point*) of what works and what doesn't.

Effectively Communicating Your Unique Value Proposition

Once you know what your unique value proposition looks like, please get into the habit of communicating your worth to others. Here are a few questions to ask yourself while preparing for this:

- **Where and when can I communicate my worth?** Some of the places where you can communicate your worth are obvious, such as interviews, appraisals, and discussions around career development. Similarly, if you're pitching your product or service to someone else, you'll likely make your unique value proposition a part of the pitch. However, there are certain places where you might have to be more proactive in communicating your value to others. For instance, if you're not used to speaking up in meetings, it's a good idea to change that. If you have trouble introducing yourself to others at networking events, you're missing out on a great opportunity to communicate your worth. Have there been instances in the past where you've been given an opportunity to talk about yourself and you've found yourself tongue-tied? Make a note of the spaces or events that you're not utilizing effectively.

- **What prevents me from communicating my worth?** Apart from missing out on opportunities or not speaking up when needed, what are the obstacles that come in the way of clear and effective communication? One of the most overlooked reasons for ineffective communication is the absence of an "elevator pitch." Simply put, an elevator pitch is a short statement that can quickly and impactfully communicate your worth to your audience. Imagine that you're trapped in an elevator with someone who could impact your career in a positive way, but you only have as much time as it takes for them to get off the elevator. Are you able to confidently and succinctly tell them who you are and how you can make things easier or better for them?

- **How can I communicate my worth?** No matter how many skills you possess or how much you've achieved so far, you need to be able to communicate them with assurance. When it comes to communication, it's as important to think about what we don't say as it is to pay attention to what we say. Not only that, but our words—impressive as they might be—have less impact than our nonverbal cues when we're interacting with others. Therefore, we need to be careful about the messages we might be subconsciously conveying to others while negotiating with them.

Building Self-Confidence and Assertiveness

Assertiveness is a quality that is key to a successful negotiation. An assertive person is sure of their competence, skills, and accomplishments and knows that they deserve a place at the table. They're able to negotiate for what they're worth and are not intimidated by others. An assertive person is also able to stay away from aggression because they don't need to resort to those tactics to get what they want. The interesting thing to note is that both diffidence and aggression stem from the same place—insecurity. While diffident people hide their insecurity by staying "invisible," aggressive people do so by making everything about themselves. Some of us might struggle with self-doubt more than others, but self-confidence is a skill that anyone can acquire with some practice.

There are four main aspects to building confidence:

- **Knowing you deserve a seat at the table:** Many women suffer from impostor syndrome in their workplace. Between dealing with workplace misogyny and being conditioned to think that we aren't really deserving of the opportunities we get or that we only get opportunities *because* we're women, many of us are hesitant to assert ourselves in various situations. Since impostor syndrome comes with feeling like an outsider most of the time, it might seem like we're the only ones dealing with it. However, it's more common than you might think, which means many people have overcome it and so can you. We've already talked about making a personal skills inventory and a value proposition statement. These can help immensely in realizing what we deserve and why we deserve it. We'll talk more about overcoming impostor syndrome in the upcoming chapters.

- **Using confident body language:** Our body language betrays how we feel more than we think. If we're slouching during a meeting, for example, it's very difficult to convince the other person that we're assured and confident in ourselves. Similarly, if we never meet the other person's eyes during a conversation, we give them the impression of being nervous or, worse, of hiding something from them. While it's clear that our body language reflects our confidence levels, the opposite is also true. If we can focus on our body language to make it look more assertive, we can signal confidence even when we don't exactly feel that way. For instance, simply maintaining good posture and gentle and consistent eye contact with the other person can go a long way in conveying confidence during our interactions.

- **Challenging yourself a little each day:** If you truly want to grow as a professional and an individual, you have to step out of your comfort zone. The good news is, you don't have to do it all at once; you can take one small step each day. If you never speak up at meetings, say, you can begin by committing to make one valid point in the next one. If you've never approached someone you think can be great for your career, start by emailing the person who intimidates you the least. Self-confidence is a muscle, and it can only work well when it's put to use regularly.

- **Acknowledging other people's qualities and achievements:** This is an extremely underrated way of building confidence and showcasing assurance to other people. Consider this: When we feel inadequate in any capacity, we tend to hyperfixate on those flaws and insecurities. Not only is that unhelpful to our journey of self-confidence, but it also alienates us from others. If, on the other hand, we can give credit where it's due and acknowledge the help and guidance of others when talking about our own accomplishments, we get out of our own heads, connect with others, and show them that we don't need to put anyone down or dismiss them in order to feel good about ourselves. If that isn't the epitome of confidence, what is?

Developing a Growth Mindset

When we talk about being assertive and overcoming impostor syndrome, our mindset makes all the difference. Psychologist and author Carol Dweck, in her book titled *Mindset: The Psychology of Success*, gave us the fascinating concept of "fixed" versus "growth" mindset. A fixed mindset essentially assumes that we are born with certain traits and capabilities, and those traits determine how we're going to do in life. Someone with a fixed mindset will say that they simply don't have the confidence needed to succeed in their career. Or if they've made a mistake on a project, they'll think to themselves *I cannot do anything right; I'm ill-suited to take on responsibilities.* This way, they sabotage their own chances of growth and success.

Someone with a growth mindset, however, will embrace the power of "yet." A growth mindset isn't about being delusional about one's abilities or overly optimistic about one's future. It's about self-awareness combined with an understanding that nothing is "fixed" in our lives. If we struggle with confidence today, it just means we haven't found our voice and leaned into our worth yet. If we've made a mistake, it just means we have more to learn, and we shouldn't give up on that project or role yet. The circumstances for both people are similar, but the person with the growth mindset sees challenges and setbacks as opportunities to grow rather than as final judgments on their performance and capability.

Here are a few things you can work on to shift from a fixed to a growth mindset:

- **Reframe challenges and setbacks as learning opportunities.** A simple yet powerful thing we can do when faced with a challenge is to focus on the lessons we've learned because of it. What has the challenge taught you about yourself? What is something you did better than expected when dealing with this setback? What is something you can work on in the future?

- **Change how you talk to yourself.** When you deal with problems at work, how do you talk to yourself? Do you give yourself grace and take a step back from the immediate problem, or do you get overwhelmed by your feelings and berate yourself? For example, when faced with a challenge, do you say something like *I'm really not up for this; I've always come up short when dealing with challenges like these*? Or do you tell yourself, *This is an opportunity to change my narrative and figure out my strengths*?

- **Embrace your humanity.** It's only when we see perfection as a goal that we have difficulty embracing a growth mindset. If we tell ourselves that we can only be perfect and nothing else, we rob ourselves of the opportunity to learn and grow in life. The chase for perfection is like chasing a mirage—it's not real, and it keeps reminding you of your thirst, of what you lack. Instead, focus on the joys of imperfection, and you'll always have something to look forward to.

- **Pay attention to your efforts.** It's close to impossible to ignore results, but we can ensure that we also pay attention to our efforts. Instead of seeing every outcome as a "win" or "loss," why not see if you've made more quality effort than before on something? Why not assess your improvement over the last time you tackled a similar project? Why not ask yourself: *Have I taken a step in the right direction?*

- **Keep asking for feedback from the right people.** The reason I say "right people" is because, while constructive criticism can help us immensely, inconsiderate or malicious criticism can deal a serious blow to our self-esteem. Therefore, once you can figure out who your true well-wishers and mentors are, ask them for honest feedback about yourself and your work. They'll likely include both your strengths and weaknesses while giving feedback, and they might also help you see opportunities that you might otherwise have missed. Genuine feedback is a great way to get out of our own heads and see ourselves through the eyes of those who wish the best for us.

Identifying and Aligning Your Values With Your Goals and Actions

A major part of embracing our worth is knowing what we stand for. Before we even move to the negotiating table, we have to be honest with ourselves about what we will fight for and what we can afford to walk away from. This is where our core values come in. As we grow and evolve in life, our beliefs and perceptions will likely shift. However, our core values are an essential part of us that don't change according to our external circumstances. These core values guide us in our personal and professional lives, making it easier for us to make decisions that align with them.

Before we move on to professional values that we would want to live by, we need to identify our personal core values. Before we do that, let's talk about what core values are. Think of it as a way of describing your truest self. Who are you? Are you courageous, honest, kind, fair, humble, or a mix of all these values? The important thing is, can you hold on to these values when times get tough? See, we all want to believe that we're courageous, but it's only when our courage is tested that we can be sure of it. Similarly, can you hold on to your integrity when you have to face adverse consequences because of it?

Determining our core values can take time, but here are a few questions that can get you started:

- *What are the most meaningful memories in my life? Why are these days meaningful to me?*

- *What are my deepest passions and how do I plan to follow them?*

- *What is something that I can fight for, even if it means opposing my friends and family members?*

- *Who are the people I look up to and why? What about them would I like to emulate in my own life? What does it tell me about my own values?*

- *What are my priorities in life? What is something I am willing to give up in order to achieve something else? What does it tell me about my core values?*

- *How would I like others to think of me when I'm not around?*

- *What would I like to be my legacy?*

- *What do I get frustrated with and would like to challenge or change around me?*

- *What about my current life makes me feel uncomfortable, and what does that tell me about the values important to me?*

Determine Work and Career Values

Before you start negotiating at work, the question you have to answer is: What am I negotiating for? And the answer isn't always obvious. On the surface, you could be negotiating for a job, a pay raise, or a role, but deep down, you're negotiating for work that aligns with your values. Of course, this is only possible if you have a clear sense of what those values are. Increasingly, workers are choosing to work for organizations that align with their values. They want to feel part of something bigger than themselves. This doesn't mean that money, security, and other more conventional needs are out of the window. It simply means that these things might not be enough anymore. Also, many of us hold on to jobs for practical reasons—like having enough money to take care of our families—and there's absolutely nothing wrong with that. At the same time, your present doesn't have to be your future. Knowing what your career values are can help you look beyond the necessities of today and focus on creating a life that makes you feel fulfilled.

Some of the common career values are reliability, respect, honesty, growth, collaboration, professionalism, and the ability to make a difference. How do you know what your career values look like? Here is a checklist you can use:

- What are your "extrinsic" motivators for choosing a job or career? These could be external or circumstantial reasons, like money or prestige.

- What are your "intrinsic" motivators for going to work? In other words, what are your reasons for working other than survival?

- What would you like to do if money wasn't a concern?

- How do you want your role or career to impact others?

- What kind of team would you like to work with, and who are your role models when it comes to mentorship and leadership?

- Where would you like to see yourself professionally in the next five years? Do you think you're on track to reach that milestone?

Align Your Career Goals With Your Values

Once you've recognized your career values, ensure that they're aligned with your career goals. The first step to take is to look at your current job and assess whether it aligns with your career goals. It's possible that this job is more about sustenance than purpose, and that's perfectly fine. Once you're aware of where you stand currently and where you want to be, you can take the following steps to bridge the gap between the two:

- Make a list of all that is missing in your current role in decreasing order of priority. This list should be able to answer the question: *What needs to change immediately for me to find purpose in my work?*

- Talk to trusted mentors about a possible change in your role or a career development path within the organization. Pay attention to whether your mentor can commit to specific timelines and provide actionable measures to help you reach your goals.

- Get into the habit of reading mission and vision statements of your current organization and other organizations you might be interested in. It's possible that the organization's mission statement is different from its actual work culture, so it's important to know what it is before you can recognize any discrepancies.

- Network with people who have worked in the organizations before you and those who are currently working in them. Ask for honest reviews and go for as many reviews as possible so that the results aren't biased.

- Once you have an idea of the kind of organization you want to work for, create a career plan for yourself. What are the aspects of your current job or role that align with this career plan, and which of them need to be changed?

- Use your values to guide you while making decisions and enforcing boundaries in your workplace.

- Wherever possible, communicate your values clearly to others in your workplace. This doesn't mean that your values will always be respected, but it will tell you all you need to know about your teammates and organization.

- Don't hesitate to ask questions when interviewing for a different role within or outside your organization. The more questions you ask, the easier it will be to assess whether the organization and role align with your career values.

Regularly Revisit and Re-Evaluate Fit

As you grow and evolve over time, your career values can also shift. For instance, as a young woman just entering the workforce, you might want to work for longer hours if it means learning the ropes in a demanding new industry.

However, over time, you might want to focus on quality over quantity and give more time to a few projects, while at the same time striking a balance between work and other commitments. As long as you know why your values have changed, you can reflect on whether the work you currently do still aligns with those values.

It's a good idea to revisit your career values at least once a year and to ask yourself certain questions about how you feel regarding your career path. Here are a few questions that can help you re-evaluate your career fit:

- *Do I feel dissatisfied with my usual roles and responsibilities?*

- *Am I feeling disconnected from my work or my colleagues?*

- *Am I struggling with feelings of self-worth and feeling confused about my identity?*

- *Do the things that made me happy or fulfilled earlier still bring me joy?*

- *Do I feel stuck in my current role or organization and yearn for a change?*

- *Does the idea of going to work fill me with boredom, anxiety, or irritation?*

Understand that your personality isn't set in stone, nor are your career goals and values. The ability to embrace what feels right to you in the moment is an act of self-love and empowerment. In this chapter, we've learned about identifying and embracing our worth.

Before we move on to the next chapter, let's revisit the exercises that can help you embrace your worth.

Exercise 1: Conduct a personal skills and achievements inventory and use them to craft a compelling personal value proposition statement.

Exercise 2: Make a list of your core values, group them according to similarity, and choose a common word or phrase that denotes them all. For example, if some of your core values are compassion, empathy, acceptance, and honesty, you could group them together as "making a positive contribution to the world." Similarly, if work–life balance, healthy living, and mindfulness are some of your core values, they can all be grouped under "living well."

In the next chapter, we will deconstruct the double bind that women have to navigate while learning to advocate for themselves.

2

Deconstructing Gender Bias—Navigating the Double Bind

"There is no limit to what we as women can accomplish."
Michelle Obama

As easy as it is to say that women should simply "ask for what they want," the truth remains that women are still navigating a world where men make most of the rules. In this world, women are expected to follow rather than lead; they're told that they're not capable of certain things—including leadership—and their worth is largely determined by those who don't know what it means to be a woman. All of this leads to a double bind that needs to be navigated by anyone who wants to be seen as a leader.

Women are often seen as poor negotiators, not because they're objectively bad at negotiation but because they're conditioned to believe that they don't possess the necessary skills for effective negotiation. Women, for instance, are usually seen as "quiet," "meek," or "soft," all of which imply that they cannot assert themselves when needed. It doesn't help that many women are asked to "stay quiet" or "avoid speaking up" because it isn't feminine or ladylike.

However, what happens when a woman decides to speak up for herself? What happens when she opposes the popular narratives about women and strives to have her voice heard? She's labeled as "difficult," "angry," "disruptive," and "disrespectful." People consider her hostile and strive to make life even more difficult for her. Unfortunately, this kind of mindset and behavior isn't limited to men. Other women who have to break out of their conditioning or who have convinced themselves that they need to appease men in order to protect their seats at the table see this woman as the problem. They've internalized the biases they have encountered throughout their lives. Therefore, that woman doesn't receive support from other women either.

This way, the "double bind" affects women negatively at the workplace, as they're made to choose between two equally unpleasant options—either stick to the script written for us by someone else or bear the consequences of deviating from the script. In this chapter, we'll explore gender bias in the workplace and how it affects us as negotiators. We'll also discuss the challenges that come with internalized biases and work on strategies to navigate this double bind during negotiations.

Understanding the Double Bind and Its Impact on Women in the Workplace

The double bind is a phenomenon that occurs when a person is confronted with two equally difficult or unhelpful choices. No matter which one they choose, they're going to be at a disadvantage. Most importantly, the person facing the double bind doesn't really have a say in the options presented to them. What makes the double bind even more sinister is that the "choices" are backed by stereotypes that are often accepted as "fact" or "truth." So, a woman "needs to be kind and soft-spoken at all times" isn't seen as a stereotype as much as a fact, which makes it all the more difficult for women to overcome that stereotype.

Let's take an example that is prevalent in many sales organizations. In general, sales is still seen as a "male" field because it's associated with aggression and confidence. In particularly cutthroat sales organizations, the motto is "sell to the customer at any and all costs." Typically, women are seen as not being up to this task. They're seen as fragile and compassionate, meaning they can neither be aggressive nor should they want to. It's assumed that women don't have it in them to do whatever it takes. What happens when a woman becomes part of a sales organization? She's usually met with doubt and pity and is given responsibilities that don't do justice to her.

What happens if the woman in question is naturally assertive and naturally takes the lead in various scenarios? If she's in a healthy environment, she'll likely be praised for taking initiative and showing promise as a sales leader, but more often than not, she'll be penalized for her behavior in ways that a man wouldn't. The strange thing is that such a woman might be seen as competent, but she won't exactly be rewarded or supported because of it. See the double bind at work? It's either "you're too feminine for this role"—which can make it easier for them to be accepted in the workplace as it reinforces a common stereotype about women—or "you're too masculine or aggressive"—which can bring results but also make the woman feel disliked or alienated.

This double bind shows up in almost every aspect of work, including negotiation. A 2011 study showed that when men were more vocal in meetings, their peers found them to be 10% more competent than men who weren't. At the same time, women who did so were seen as 14% less competent than women who didn't (Brescoll, 2011). This is likely because for men, speaking up and asserting themselves through their ideas is seen as the norm, which means someone who keeps quiet is either not smart or not confident enough. Women, on the other hand, are conditioned to follow and keep their opinions to themselves, so someone who speaks up is usually seen as being disruptive and adding nothing to the conversation.

Historical and Cultural Context of Gender Stereotypes

Gender bias does not exist in a vacuum, and there are both historical and cultural reasons for these stereotypes to be prevalent even today. To begin with, patriarchy has been a part of most cultures across the world, which means that children are introduced to damaging gender roles very early on. It starts with messages like, "This is not how girls behave" or "That job is not worthy of boys." Girls are told they can only play with dolls, dress in certain ways, and talk in a manner that doesn't upset or offend anyone. While this is bad enough, boys don't have it easy either.

Boys are asked to be "tough" and "masculine," to "not cry like girls," and to choose only among tasks and jobs that are suited to their masculinity. Since gender stereotypes seem almost universal, it can be difficult for children to grow up believing that there are other possibilities for them in the world. What's more, these ideas are constantly reinforced by the world around them.

The social learning theory—introduced by Albert Bandura in the 1960s—tells us that children learn which behaviors are appropriate and which aren't based on whether they are rewarded or punished for them. For instance, if a boy wants to go into something that is traditionally seen as a woman's domain—say, he's interested in being a homemaker—he will be ridiculed, punished, and ostracized for his choices. It's likely that his parents and other adults will also participate in punishing him because they don't want him to face challenges later on in life or because they truly believe he's going down the wrong path. Similarly, children look up to the adults in their lives when they want to learn more about gender roles. In families and education systems where these roles are rigidly adhered to, children grow up internalizing these misleading messages.

Another theory that helps us understand how gender stereotypes begin early on and persist through adulthood is the gender schema theory, introduced by Sandra Bem in 1981. It tells us that cultural and social norms play a vital role in how children and even adults organize and recollect information related to gender roles and differences. If a child has been taught or shown examples of strict gender roles, they'll likely remember that information for a long time. For example, if an adult is shown pictures of male and female doctors—and they've been told that women are not cut out for the medical field—they'll likely remember or identify with only the male doctor. When it comes to nurses, their reaction will likely be the opposite. So, they not only seek out confirmation of their biases, but they also reject any information that might challenge this bias. This theory also gives us a clue about how even women can internalize certain harmful biases regarding their own competence and worth (more on this soon).

What are some of these common "misrepresentations" that contribute to the double bind for women in workplaces and elsewhere?

- **Leaders are usually portrayed as masculine, with traits like charisma, aggression, and confidence.** This means that women are seen as followers who don't question the leaders and who don't have any special characteristics of their own.

- **Women are seen as nurturing, empathetic, and compassionate—qualities that are not traditionally related to leadership.** Since a leader needs to make difficult decisions, it's assumed that women don't have what it takes to do what needs to be done.

- **Women are seen as compliant and agreeable.** When women head negotiations, they're expected to agree to the other party's demands without much resistance. Therefore, they're usually seen as being unfit for negotiations, but when they do stick to their fair demands, they're seen as difficult or arrogant.

Consequences of Gender Bias in Negotiations

When it comes to negotiations, gender stereotypes create a lose-lose situation for everyone. Let's discuss some of these consequences in this section.

Economic Outcomes of Gender Bias in Negotiations

Research has shown that men, on average, tend to perform better in negotiations than women. However, the interesting bit is that women perform better when negotiating for others but not so well when negotiating for themselves. The reason for this is that women are taught to prioritize other people's needs over their own. So they don't worry about backlash or resistance when trying to help others, but when it comes to their own needs, they're conditioned to back down quickly (Shonk, 2024c).

Since women have difficulty negotiating well for themselves, it also has an impact on their career progression. This inability to negotiate effectively for themselves has at least some role to play in the gender wage gap in many industries. Similarly, women are often hesitant to ask for raises, promotions, or even roles that would be better suited to their capabilities. In many cases, women need extra support—especially if they're mothers or caregivers—and flexibility to do well in their roles.

However, they often don't ask for additional support because they're worried about the backlash they will receive—not only from their seniors but also from their own colleagues. In fact, many more women than men face negative reviews related to their behaviors. This is because the same kind of behaviors that are accepted in men—including, but not limited to, anger, confidence, and confrontational behaviors—are chastised in women. As a result, fewer women progress in their careers to break the proverbial glass ceiling, and many women drop out of the workforce when they find it difficult to justify the effort they have to put in for subpar results in terms of economic and career security.

Differences in Negotiation Strategies and Behaviors

Since women are expected to be understanding and agreeable, they usually stay away from assertive negotiation tactics. When women do assert themselves, they're mistaken for being aggressive, which makes it even more difficult for them to hold on to their actual needs and beliefs.

Consequently, when it comes to negotiating with someone who holds more power over them, women usually back off earlier or are eager to agree with the other party. Contrast this with how men behave even when the other person is more powerful than them, and we can see that power dynamics affect women more negatively during negotiations, even when they shouldn't. Since women are made to be acutely aware of the power disparity between them and men in society, they find themselves struggling to assert themselves when dealing with people in power at the workplace.

Perceptions and Social Backlash

It can sometimes feel like women cannot win, no matter what they do. If they don't negotiate well, they're seen as being unworthy of tough and demanding situations. If they do, they are called "off-putting" or "combative" by their peers and seniors alike. When men get angry or intense in the course of negotiations, they're mostly given a pass because that's how they're supposed to be. On the other hand, if women stand their ground and refuse to budge, they receive a lot of criticism for the same. Think of how a strict boss at the workplace is perceived if they're a man and how those perceptions change if they're a woman.

Most importantly, however, these stereotypes harm women and their organizations by convincing the women that their success depends less on their negotiation skills and more on the roles determined for them by society. At the end of the day, negotiation is a skill that isn't inherently gender-dependent. Sure, the way society perceives us can have an effect on our motivation levels as well as on the outcomes in certain circumstances, but we do more harm to ourselves by internalizing these harmful stereotypes and repeating what we've always heard from others: *We simply don't have what it takes to be successful negotiators.*

Recognizing and Challenging Internalized Biases

Till now, we've seen that it's not just men who believe that women deserve less at the workplace (and even in other aspects of life) but women themselves who ridicule and criticize women who fight for a seat at the table. If a woman manages to become a leader, she faces extra scrutiny not only from men but also from women. What's worse is that, in many cases, women undermine their own strengths and fail to advocate for themselves. The trope "women are their own worst enemy" seems like a way for patriarchal institutions to deflect their own responsibility for the challenges that women seem to face everywhere, but there's at least some truth behind it.

To understand this phenomenon better, we need to recognize the three kinds of sexism that we might encounter on a daily basis. One of them is institutional sexism, which refers to the prevalence of patriarchal thought and beliefs in various aspects of our lives. For example, institutional sexism can affect the policies at our workplace, influence our access to education, employment opportunities, and healthcare, and even affect the decisions we can make for ourselves.

The second kind of sexism is interpersonal sexism, where one person can act in sexist ways while interacting with us. Their thoughts and behaviors are affected by the prevalence of institutional sexism around them, but they can also be the result of their own thoughts and experiences. For instance, someone who resents a woman for performing better than them at work can resort to sexist remarks and microaggressions that make her feel isolated and disrespected at the workplace. They could hint to their colleagues that the woman in question has not achieved any success on her own merit but rather because she's being given unfair advantages due to her gender. Interpersonal sexism can be as subtle as it is damaging.

The third kind of sexism is internalized sexism, which can sneak up on any woman who has witnessed the effects of both institutional and interpersonal sexism all her life. When sexism begins to seem like the norm, it feels pointless to question the patriarchal systems that lead to it and blame those who are trying to fight these systems. Similarly, instead of seeing patriarchy for what it is, women begin to accept its damaging messages as truth and become hostile toward anyone who tries to help them break free. This is why it can be easier to believe that *I'm not good at negotiation*, that *I don't have the confidence to ask for what I want*, or even that *I don't deserve any of the things I want*, rather than giving yourself grace and acknowledging that you've been receiving sexist messages all your life.

Another aspect of internalized bias in women is that women tend to compete among themselves rather than challenge the systems that keep them from having equal opportunities at the workplace. Why is it that there are limited positions for women or that only one woman can be a part of a particular team? Why do women have to view each other as enemies while vying for positions or negotiating raises instead of trying to dismantle the system together?

Recognizing these biases is the first step toward overcoming them, but how do we know whether we have internalized them? Here is a checklist that can help you do so:

- Do you have any preconceived notions about how men and women are *supposed to* behave or what qualities men and women possess?

- Do you think women can be "too ambitious" or "too loud," and would you say the same things for men?

- Do you think women need to behave in certain ways so that they aren't targeted by men? For example, is the woman responsible for how a man behaves with her in the workplace?

- Do you think that men achieve things on their own merit while women usually benefit from unfair advantages or by "playing the woman card?"

- Do you believe that women are inherently bad at some things or that they're wired in ways that keep them from achieving certain milestones?

- Do you feel like you need to prioritize other people's needs and feelings over your own, or else you're a selfish person?

- Do you feel guilty about asking for something you want—including a raise, a promotion, or a different kind of project?

- Do you think you're being "difficult" at times when you want to advocate for yourself or assert yourself in the workplace?

- Do you believe that there's only so much you can do to overcome gender bias in the workplace?

- Do you think it's easier to "go with the flow" than to make waves at your workplace?

- Do you sometimes feel resentful when a woman seems to "have it easy?"

- Do you have difficulty setting individualistic goals for yourself? Do you think that your goals should include the needs of other people?

- Do you sometimes act like your goals are too high or out-of-reach as a woman?

- Do you feel ashamed when talking about your achievements?

- Do you feel like downplaying your contributions to the team or organization in order to come across as humble?

It's possible that some of these questions trigger you or make you feel bad about letting yourself down. That's not the intention of this exercise. If anything, these questions should make you feel more comfortable about confronting your internalized bias. The important thing is to be kind to yourself for all the ways you've given up on yourself in the past and to use these insights to change the narrative going forward.

Strategies for Overcoming Internalized Gender Expectations in Negotiations

Here are a few strategies for overcoming internalized gender bias in negotiations:

- **Reflect on your internalized biases and understand what they mean for you.** Your internalized biases are telling you something important about your environment, culture, and beliefs. Coming face-to-face with our biases can be unsettling and upsetting, but these biases can tell us exactly what we need to improve in order to better advocate for ourselves. For example, a recent study concluded that when male and female negotiators were compared with each other, they both showed similar tendencies to recognize opportunities for negotiation. However, while men in general felt entitled to better opportunities and higher pay, women experienced greater apprehension while negotiating. This led to men negotiating at higher levels while women negotiated at much lower levels, if at all (Mozahem et al., 2021).

- **Challenge these stereotypes when you can.** We need to recognize that our internalized biases are a reflection of institutional sexism, but it's also crucial to not feel helpless in the face of it. It's not possible to change the system overnight, but it's possible that you have more power than you might think. For example, if you are in a position to work with a team of people new to the workforce, you can influence them to challenge their own beliefs about women as negotiators. You can also set an example for them by challenging some of your biases as well.

- **Reframe how you see negotiation.** We'll be talking a lot about this throughout the book because so much of effective negotiation has to do with our mindset. As a starting point, it helps to understand that aggression and entitlement aren't great ways to approach a negotiation. Negotiation involves both parties understanding each other and their needs and coming to a win-win solution. Instead of seeing yourself as a poor negotiator, maybe consider that you've been looking at the art of negotiation in a different light.

- **Develop your negotiation skills.** While it's true that your environment will have an impact on your negotiations, there are skills you can learn and practice in order to improve yourself. Instead of selling yourself short or giving in to despair, why not focus on what you can learn and what will empower you while negotiating for yourself and others?

- **Build your support network.** In this chapter, we've seen how gender stereotypes related to negotiation become more accepted over time through cultural and social support. To counter this, women need more allies—both male and female—who can support them and show them that a different reality is possible. For those of us who have battled internalized gender bias for most of our lives, meeting people who "prove us wrong" can feel like finally getting out of our heads and being able to take action. Let's talk more about the importance of support networks in the next section.

Sponsors and Mentors: Building a Support Network

When negotiating for themselves, women face two major challenges: the gender expectations of those around them and their own internalized biases. To overcome these challenges, they need allies—people within or even outside their organizations who help and support them when needed. In general, allies can be male or female, and in traditional organizations, there's a greater chance of having male allies than female ones, purely because of how many more of them are present in managerial and senior leadership positions. However, as more and more women break the glass ceiling and take on leadership roles, there's a greater chance for women to find other women allies in their organizations and industries.

There are two main types of allies we need in our professional lives—mentors and sponsors. Both mentors and sponsors empower women in their careers but in different ways. A mentor is one who provides the necessary guidance and motivation to women to overcome their internalized biases and to develop themselves professionally. A mentor can be found either within or outside your current organization. Since a mentor has reached a certain position in their career after facing several challenges, they can act as a role model for the woman who is just starting out or who needs added support in her career. This is also why it's useful if your mentors (and sponsors) are women, because they know exactly how it feels to be in the position you are currently in.

Mentors are also instrumental in helping you develop your skills, create a road map for your career progression, and give you advice about balancing your life and career. This can be very useful for women because they usually have to balance their caregiving duties with their career aspirations. Last but not least, mentors can introduce you to their own networks, thus giving you much-needed exposure as well as opening you up to opportunities that might not have come to you otherwise.

Sponsors, on the other hand, are normally found within the organization and are in positions of power. A mentor can also hold a position of power, but they don't have to necessarily use their influence to further your career. A sponsor, however, does exactly that. They ensure that you are visible to those who matter within the organization, that you get access to the resources needed to advance your career, and that your performance is highlighted and lauded in the right spaces. A sponsor takes an active role in your career and, in a sense, advocates for you by putting their own reputation on the line. After all, sponsors hold themselves accountable for the success of their sponsees, which also means that the sponsee needs to do their very best to prove their sponsors right.

The Role of Mentorship and Sponsorship in Fighting Gender Bias

There are many ways in which mentorship and sponsorship help fight gender bias:

- **They tell us what's truly possible.** Simply by listening to the stories our mentors and sponsors tell us, we can begin to overcome our internalized biases. We can get out of a "fixed" or "victim" mindset by pushing ourselves to see beyond our setbacks and challenges. They also serve as real-life examples of success despite obstacles.

- **They help balance opportunities with risks.** Mentors and sponsors can both help us become more aware of opportunities around us, but they also help mitigate the risk that comes with negotiating for ourselves and making big leaps in our careers. Remember, we talked about how negotiating and advocating for ourselves can sometimes result in backlash? If we have mentors and sponsors who support us and who are willing to advocate for us in front of their peers, it can help mitigate this backlash.

- **They can help bring about a cultural change in the organization.**

As more and more women reach leadership positions and offer to be mentors and sponsors to those just entering the workforce, they create a culture of women empowerment and collaboration within the workplace. They also help others challenge their own biases about women negotiators and create a culture where women are given equal opportunities to prove their worth.

- **They can help the organization overcome the "broken rung" phenomenon.** This term was coined by Sheryl Sandberg and McKinsey in a joint study where they found out that men and women who entered the organization at the same position were often treated very differently when they started to progress in their careers (Field et al., 2023). On average, men were more likely to be promoted than women for managerial positions, which meant fewer women were available to be considered for leadership roles later on. Mentors and sponsors help repair this broken rung by preparing and advocating more women for managerial roles and by influencing hiring decisions in a favorable manner.

Strategies for Seeking Out and Building Mentoring Relationships

While we can and should try to seek sponsors as well, they're usually harder to find in the beginning. Also, a sponsor might need some assurance—either in terms of consistent performance or from your mentor—before they throw their weight behind you. Therefore, we first need to learn how to find and build mentoring relationships before we move on to sponsorships. Here are a few steps you can take to find a good mentor for yourself:

- **Take some time to figure out your goals and expectations.** Why do you desire a mentor in your life? What kind of mentor do you need, and how would that mentor help you achieve your career goals? If you aren't clear about what you want, you'll likely waste both your and your mentor's time in the future. So, before you reach out to anyone, figure out what you want from your career and from the relationship.

- **Do your research on your prospective mentors.** Make sure to know what they are passionate about and how they can help you. What is it that they're looking for in mentees, and what about them makes them a good fit for this relationship? You won't be able to know everything about them, but some basic research is warranted before you approach them. This will also help you create a compelling pitch for when you communicate with them for the first time.

- **Widen your search to ensure you meet a mentor who will enrich your career.** Start with your immediate professional network and move on to other organizations in the industry. You can also look for professional organizations that specialize in matching mentors with prospective mentees.

- **Take the initiative and reach out to them.** You can start by asking them to meet you for some time so you can tell them exactly why you think they would be a great mentor to you. Your previous research and your value proposition statement can help you at this stage. Remember that your mentor will likely be a busy professional themselves, so the clearer you are while communicating with them, the more they'll value their relationship with you.

- **Come up with a schedule that works for both of you.** If you and your mentor get along really well, you'll likely be a part of each other's journey for a long time. However, it's important to initially decide on a schedule that helps both of you show up consistently for the relationship. For instance, you could decide to meet once every two weeks for the next six months and then review your relationship after those six months have ended. You could also decide the duration and agenda for each subsequent meeting.

- **Ensure that it is a mutually valuable relationship.** As mentees, we often make the mistake of leaning too heavily on our mentors. You might feel like you cannot really provide value to your mentor, but you never know until you've asked them. Your conversations should enrich them in some way, and even if you cannot help them per se, you should not make mentoring feel like a chore to them. For example, don't treat your mentor as your therapist, and always check in with them to make sure they're in the right frame of mind to listen to you and offer advice.

- **Provide mentorship wherever possible.** One of the best ways to thank your mentor is by paying it forward. Look for people who might need guidance and offer your time and wisdom to them. Let the people in your organization know that you're willing to provide mentorship to others. This is also a great way to show up as an "unofficial" leader in your organization.

When it comes to sponsors, the steps are pretty much the same, except that the relationship is more formal, short-lived, and one-dimensional. This doesn't mean that your sponsor cannot also become your mentor over time, but their role as a sponsor is to connect you to the right opportunities and people. A great way to connect with sponsors is through your mentor. Apart from doing good work and looking for people who can advocate for you, you can also ask your mentor to suggest a good sponsor based on what they know about you and your capabilities.

Before we move on to the next chapter, let's analyze a double bind scenario and learn how to navigate it.

Double Bind Scenario Analysis

Let's understand the double bind in detail through the following scenario:

Scenario: Salary negotiation for a job offer.

Situation: Sania is a brilliant software engineer who has been working in the industry for about seven years and has racked up a great resume during this time. She likes her current job but also feels ready for something more challenging. She puts out feelers and soon receives interest from some exciting organizations. One of these roles seems entirely up her alley and she cannot wait to start, but the compensation she's being offered by the organization seems to be low as compared to her qualifications and years of experience. In fact, she knows a couple of male colleagues of hers who have received higher offers for similar roles in the organization.

Why it is a double bind: Sania knows that she deserves more than she's being offered currently, but years of working in the tech industry has taught her the importance of getting along with people. She knows she would not have made it so far in her career if she were deemed as "difficult" or "aggressive," which is why she isn't sure about how to negotiate a higher salary without coming across as ungrateful or confrontational.

Discussion questions:

- What are the challenges Sania might face while negotiating for a higher salary?

- What role does gender bias play in this scenario? How can the biases of the employers and colleagues affect the process and outcome of the negotiation?

- Do Sania's own biases play a role in how she deals with this situation?

- How can Sania bridge the gap between "knowing her worth" and "communicating her worth" in an effective manner?

Tips for dealing with the double bind situation:

- **Pay attention to the language used by Sania** when negotiating for a higher salary. Move away from "accusatory" or "aggressive" language and work on framing her needs in an objective manner.

- Think about how the negotiation can become a **win-win situation** by focusing not just on what Sania deserves but also on what she can contribute to the organization she's going to join. So, instead of "this is what I deserve," can it be "this is what we can offer each other?"

- Focus on **certain aspects of Sania's career that she might not be utilizing** while negotiating with her future employers. For example, can she ask a mentor or a trusted colleague to publicly recommend her as a way of conveying her value to her future organization?

Spend some time with this scenario and think about similar scenarios in your own life. Think about what you could have done better and how your own biases might be stopping you from asking for what you truly deserve. We'll now move on to the strategies and techniques that can help us master the art of negotiation.

PART 2:
INVESTIGATE OPPORTUNITIES

3

Mastering the Art of Negotiation—Strategies and Techniques

"The most difficult thing in any negotiation, almost, is making sure that you strip it of the emotion and deal with the facts."
Howard Baker

In the last chapter, we talked about the importance of reframing negotiations in order to be successful at them. The general consensus seems to be that "masculine" qualities are necessary for women to succeed at negotiations, which can be a bit misleading for a number of reasons. One, the qualities needed for negotiations aren't inherently masculine or feminine, though men might be conditioned to develop those qualities while women are discouraged from doing so.

More importantly, negotiation isn't a game of emotions or egos. It's not about proving yourself to the other party, nor is it about "tricking" them into getting what you want. Yes, when we're negotiating for something, we're usually attached to the conclusion, and that's perfectly normal. For instance, if you're negotiating for better working conditions or a more flexible schedule at your workplace, you're negotiating for your peace of mind, work-life balance, and the possibility to stay in your current role for longer. However, even when the stakes are high, they don't need to overpower our ability to stick to the facts and think through our decisions.

Ultimately, negotiation is a tool to get what you want by creating opportunities for the other party. No one wants to walk away from a negotiation feeling like they've received the short end of the stick. Also, negotiation is as much an art as it is a skill. Many people mistakenly assume that you can either be great at negotiation or terrible at it, which couldn't be further from the truth. Instead of getting bogged down by the gender bias that pervades this discussion, we need to empower ourselves by learning about the various strategies and techniques that can help us become better at negotiation.

Preparing for a Successful Negotiation

When we stop looking at negotiation as an innate ability, we can help ourselves and the other party by preparing for successful negotiations. In this section, we'll talk about the steps we can take to prepare ourselves before taking a seat at the table.

Self-Assessment and Goal Setting

You cannot be successful as a negotiator if you do not know yourself, your strengths and weaknesses, and your needs. In the first chapter, we've talked about the importance of crafting a personal value proposition statement, as it helps us determine what it is that we're "fighting for." Similarly, you must decide beforehand what your goals are and what you hope to achieve through the negotiation. Here are a few prompts that can help you at this stage:

- *Why is this negotiation important to me?*

- *What* do I expect from this negotiation?

- *What are my strengths and weaknesses going into this negotiation?*

- *What makes me confident about achieving my negotiation goals?*

Market Research and Benchmarking

You cannot be successful at negotiation if you don't know what you're up against and what the market looks like at the time. For instance, if you're looking for a salary hike, you should have an idea of how much the organization pays its current employees for similar roles and how these salaries compare with the rest of the industry. There are two main reasons why good market research makes all the difference, especially for women. When women don't have access to proper information about the minimum and maximum limits within which they can negotiate, they tend to focus more on the biases that hold them back. Being informed about what is going on in the industry or organization helps them negotiate logically and dispassionately. Another reason for doing proper research is that it allows us to reframe our individual goals as shared ones. It helps us understand what the other party needs and tailor our strategy based on that knowledge.

Gathering Supporting Data

Once you've decided what your negotiation goal is and what limits you can set for them, the next step is to gather data that supports your "ask." Remember that your ask cannot be centered only around yourself but should also take into account what the other party wants. For example, a salary hike cannot only be "I deserve this because I've done great work in the past," but "This salary hike allows me to work for your organization and feel valued, which means I will do my best work and help you achieve your [insert specific goals of the organization]."

Depending on the situation, you can also collect data about certain relevant trends that might affect the outcome of the negotiation. For example, if you're negotiating with a potential client about trying to sell a premium product in the market, you'll need to convince them that it's a good idea. To do this, you can share data on existing premium products in the market and their performance over the last year or so. Similarly, your data can show the client that a premium product can justify its cost by lasting longer.

Developing Your Negotiation Strategy

There are two things to keep in mind while preparing for negotiation: your negotiation style and your negotiation strategy. Knowing what kind of negotiator you are—beyond sexist stereotypes—can help you determine if your style is appropriate for a particular scenario. The same goes for the strategy you use during negotiation. Perhaps the most underrated piece of advice when it comes to negotiation is that we should treat each scenario as unique. This is where your research about the organization and/or person will come in handy.

There are some scenarios where it might be useful to let the other party begin so that you can assess them and tweak your own strategy accordingly. Then there are situations where you might need to assert yourself in the beginning. Do you want to clearly state your intentions and expectations beforehand, or do you want the other party to reveal a bit about themselves by giving them a chance to talk? Your strategy should be prepared beforehand, but it shouldn't be rigid.

Enhancing Your Communication Skills

When it comes to negotiation, what you say is as important as how you say it. Since both parties are trying to come to a win-win solution, it's vital that our verbal and nonverbal cues align with our intentions. We should also remember that the stakes are usually high in a negotiation, and both parties can be a bit on the edge during this time. Hence, we cannot afford to be careless while communicating with them, as miscommunication of any kind can be perceived as condescension. When working on our communication skills, we often forget that "listening" is as much a part of the process as "talking," and it might even be the more powerful one. We'll talk more about it soon.

Preparing for Different Outcomes

Often, negotiations are presented as either successful or unsuccessful, meaning you either get what you want or you walk away from the negotiating table. While in some cases, it might be necessary to walk away, there's another option we can explore. We can create a list of alternatives that will work in case our primary goal is not met. If possible, we can also prepare ourselves for more than one outcome so that we don't get overwhelmed or flustered when things don't go our way. We'll talk more about this in the next section.

Practicing Your Pitch

Whether you feel confident about your pitch or not, you should practice it as much as possible before sitting down for negotiations. Not only will this help you perfect your delivery and enhance your confidence, but it will also help you notice any pitfalls beforehand. If you can, practice your pitch with someone who is familiar with the scenario and who can give you constructive feedback to work on. The aim is not to sound like you've memorized a script but to be as prepared as possible on the day of negotiations.

Preparing Yourself Mentally and Emotionally

Negotiations can and often do get heated, simply because both parties want their own needs fulfilled. Also, women can feel targeted or disrespected during a negotiation, subtly or otherwise. Sometimes, no matter how hard we try, our internal biases overwhelm us, which can make us behave in a self-defeating manner. Therefore, we need to prepare ourselves mentally and emotionally before we begin negotiations. Here are a few things that can help:

- **Acknowledge your emotions before and during the negotiation.** Since we're expected to keep our emotions at bay not only during negotiations but in almost all aspects of work, we get trapped in a cycle of guilt and shame whenever we experience difficult emotions. Between repressing our emotions—which isn't healthy and can lead to outbursts at the worst possible times—and giving in to them, there's an often unexplored option: acknowledging how we're feeling without getting overwhelmed by those emotions. If you can simply take a deep breath or three and then tell yourself that your emotions are valid, you'll feel calmer and more in control of those emotions.

- **It's okay to be a little anxious, but don't let it consume you.** The outcomes of negotiations are important to us, so it's normal to feel anxious, but too much anxiety can keep us from performing well. This is another reason why practicing regularly before the negotiation helps us. Simple mindfulness techniques like deep breathing, grounding ourselves, and checking in regularly to see how our bodies are reacting to the situation can help us be more mindful and less anxious during negotiations.

- **Keep your focus on the problem.** If you can see the negotiation as a shared problem that needs a solution, you'll be less likely to take things personally during the process. Make sure you've clearly defined the problem so that you can remind yourself what you're fighting for in the first place.

- **Make sure you're not preoccupied on the day of negotiations.** While we cannot anticipate everything, we can prepare ourselves by focusing as much as possible on the negotiation. Keep distractions at bay and be present at all times. This is especially important for women because, at any given time, we're likely thinking about work, home, children (if we have them), and a myriad other responsibilities we might be juggling.

Defining Your Best Alternative to a Negotiated Agreement

In the previous section, we've discussed that we should prepare for different outcomes during a negotiation. Your best alternative to a negotiated agreement (BATNA) is a great tool that ensures you negotiate confidently and achieve success while negotiating. This concept was first introduced by William Ury and Roger Fisher in the 1981 book *Getting to Yes: Negotiation Agreement Without Giving In*. Let's take an example to understand what a BATNA looks like. Suppose you're looking for a salary hike and your current organization isn't giving you as much as you would like. So, you start looking for roles elsewhere and land a couple offers that are offering salary hikes; however, one of these organizations isn't giving you your dream role, while another organization isn't as great at providing work-life balance as you might like. So, you have three options at this point:

1. Accept the salary hike being offered by your current organization.

2. Accept a salary hike at the second organization, but compromise on your current role.

3. Accept a salary hike at the third organization, but compromise on your work-life balance.

Now, it's time to evaluate whether the salary hike is more important than having a work-life balance or your dream role. At first glance, you might feel like your organization is offering you the best of all worlds, but this doesn't have to be true. For example, if you try to find out more about the role you're being offered at the second organization, you might begin to see the merits of that role. You might also learn that you can use that role to negotiate a better position within the organization in the next year or so. Therefore, in the long term, it might be a better option than you once thought. While work-life balance is extremely important to you, you might also find that you can work a bit more for the next couple of years so that your salary base increases. Now, you have three options instead of one, and they can be very useful in negotiating for what you want.

Importance of Having a Strong BATNA

Having a strong BATNA can be useful for us in several ways:

- **It provides a safety net during negotiations.** Without a strong BATNA, we have only two options: accept what the other party offers or walk away from negotiations. Having alternatives helps us negotiate without feeling pressured or insecure.

- **It helps us be more assertive during negotiations.** When we know we have other options, we naturally feel more confident and can assert ourselves during the negotiations. In fact, we have no reason to get aggressive when we're not desperate to have the other party accept our terms. This gives us a solid edge over the other party.

- **It helps us make better decisions.** When we're clear about the alternatives we have, it becomes easier to think rationally rather than emotionally. We also become clear on what we can and cannot accept during the negotiations, which makes it easier to stick to our decisions when things aren't going our way.

- **It is an empowering situation to be in.** For women especially, negotiations can seem like a place where we're giving away our power—not least because the other party may have preconceived notions about us. A strong BATNA allows us to level the playing field by giving us a reason to walk away if needed and helping us form data-based arguments during the negotiation. Also, women tend to become better at negotiations the more time they spend at the negotiating table, as that gives them the time needed to learn about the other party and to tweak their own behaviors accordingly. This is something that a strong BATNA allows us—time and perspective.

- **It can help preserve relationships.** This can sound counterintuitive, so stay with me as I explain it. While there are some negotiations that are purely transactional in nature, most negotiations work on the principle of maintaining relationships. This is also why a good negotiation is about creating win-win solutions so that neither party walks away feeling betrayed or disrespected. When one party compromises too much or lets the other party get their way, they can feel resentful about it in the long term. Similarly, if someone is too aggressive and insists on getting their own way, they risk jeopardizing a long-term relationship for a single victory. When we have a BATNA, we're able to work on getting our way without negatively compromising the other party's needs.

Strategies for Developing and Leveraging Your BATNA

Here are some things to keep in mind while developing your BATNA:

- **Know your purpose behind selecting a BATNA.** Be clear about what you want the negotiation to achieve. For example, if you want a salary hike at any cost, then you might have to walk away if your organization refuses to budge. If you're working on a negotiation deal with other stakeholders, consult with them and make sure everyone is on the same page regarding these goals.

- **Research and prepare as thoroughly as possible.** Just as with any other aspect of the negotiation, proper preparation ensures that you're not caught unawares during the process. The more you research, the more possibilities you'll be able to find in your proposal.

- **List and evaluate alternatives.** Remember that your BATNA can also fall through, just like your main option, so it's best to have at least two to three options available beforehand. The more options you have, the greater your bargaining power. Each alternative needs to be evaluated carefully before you make it a part of your official proposal. For example, if you've received a very high salary offer from an organization but their work culture leaves much to be desired, it cannot be a part of your BATNA.

- **Improve your BATNA by asking for opinions and widening your scope.** Get other people's perspectives on your BATNA and consider as many alternatives as possible before deciding on them. If you feel like your BATNA can be improved, do so. If you think that there's a scope of getting a different role along with the salary hike in the second organization, for example, negotiate with them before you include it in your BATNA. At the end of the day, your BATNA should be actionable, practical, and attractive, or it will cause more harm than good.

- **Keep the other party in mind as well.** Understand this: You're only considering your BATNA because you want to negotiate with the other party. Meaning, if you didn't want a salary hike within your organization, you wouldn't be looking for alternatives outside of it. This means that your organization's needs are also important. So, a BATNA is not just about being able to walk away if needed; it's also about possibly reaching an agreement with the other party. So, make sure your BATNA is respectful of their needs, and understand that they can have their own BATNA as well. Just because you have options doesn't mean you underestimate what the other party might have.

Leveraging Your BATNA

There are some things to keep in mind while leveraging your BATNA:

- **Communicate it as clearly and honestly as possible.** Your BATNA only has power if it is communicated with the other party. Make sure that your BATNA is as clear and succinct as possible. It should also be accurate, because if the other party figures out you're bluffing, you risk losing not only the current negotiation but also your relationship with them. For example, it's not a great idea to inflate the salary you're being offered just to make your position stronger.

- **Timing is important too.** Sometimes, it can be helpful to start the negotiations by stating your BATNA, but in most cases, you need to figure out when to introduce it. Usually, a good time to introduce your BATNA is when talks have stalled and you've reached an impasse. Make sure there's some scope of negotiating further when you introduce your BATNA, or else the other party will have already made their mind up at this stage.

- **Your BATNA should not sound like a threat but rather as an opportunity.** This one is difficult to achieve, mostly because having multiple options can sometimes make us impatient and even inconsiderate of the other party's needs. Therefore, when you're talking about the salary hike being offered, instead of saying something like, "I have a much better offer from another organization," you can say, "I really like working here, which is why I would love it if you could reconsider some of my terms. A salary hike will give me the assurance needed to give more to the role and the organization that I truly cherish."

- **Don't be rigid about your BATNA.** Remember that your

organization likely has its own BATNA as well. For example, they could also be considering some candidates to take over your role if negotiations fall through. If you truly love the role and the organization, you might also have to make some compromises and look for ways to reach a middle ground.

- **Know when you cannot bargain any further.** A strong BATNA allows us to stay at the negotiating table for longer and preferably find something that works for both parties. However, each party has a higher and lower limit. The lower limit signifies the most they can compromise on before the deal loses its feasibility for them. You should know this limit before you walk into the negotiation. If, for example, you need at least a 15% salary hike to justify staying in your current organization, you'll have to walk away if the other party tries to go lower than this.

The Power of Empathy and Active Listening in Negotiation

When we're talking about gender roles and biases in negotiation, we often focus on the negative aspects and forget that women can also bring their own strengths to the table. While empathy and active listening are certainly not "feminine" traits, women are conditioned to listen and pay attention to other people's needs rather than voice their own. Also, women find it easier to be in touch with their feelings and to allow other women to express themselves in their presence. Men, on the other hand, are often asked to be "in control of their emotions" and to repress how they feel as much as possible. As a result, women find it easier to be empathetic and active listeners. Fortunately for us, these are amazing qualities to have during negotiations.

The ability to empathize with the other party during negotiations means that we don't aim for a win-lose solution and that we have greater chances of salvaging our relationship even after tough negotiations. Empathy isn't the same as pity; it simply means that you honor and acknowledge the other person's needs along with your own. Active listening is a skill very closely related to empathy. An active listener doesn't listen just to speak; they don't pretend to pay attention while impatiently waiting for their own turn. Rather, they realize the value of letting the other person express themselves without being judged or interrupted, and they welcome the opportunity to know more about the person or organization they're negotiating with.

There are two main reasons why active listening is important during negotiations. One, when we listen carefully to what the other party is saying, we often get more information than we bargained for. Making the other party comfortable enough to tell us details they hadn't even accounted for is a great way to know where we truly stand during the process. Two, when we show the other party that we're keen on listening to them, we convey respect and consideration even if we're sitting on opposite sides of the proverbial table. You'd be surprised by how much can be achieved simply by giving people space to express themselves. Think of it as giving the other party the signal that what they're saying is extremely important to you—because it is.

Here are a few ways in which you can practice active listening and build rapport with the other party:

- **Make sure you're fully present during negotiations.** This ties into the earlier point of mindfulness during negotiations. The first thing to do is to eliminate distractions as much as you can. You might need to take a call or respond to a message if it is an emergency, but keep your phone and other digital devices away from you otherwise. When talking to the other person, communicate your interest and presence by maintaining steady but gentle eye contact. The idea is to connect with them, not to intimidate them or give them the impression that you're bored. When the other person is speaking, keep your interruptions to a minimum.

- **Demonstrate empathy, especially through nonverbal cues.** It is essential to show the other person that you understand their needs, which can be communicated through powerful nonverbal and limited verbal cues. For example, simply nodding along and smiling every now and then (at appropriate moments, of course) should give them the confidence that you're not an enemy and can become their ally. Similarly, an open body posture communicates trust and warmth, while a closed body posture—such as crossing your arms and legs—can communicate impatience and distrust. When the other person is speaking, you should keep your own words to a minimum, but if you have to say something, use one or two sentences to validate what they're saying. If the other party tells you that the market is very tough for them right now, let them know you hear them and agree with them.

- **Use paraphrasing in an effective manner.** Once the other person is done speaking, you can paraphrase what they said to convey to them that you were listening. Paraphrasing isn't only about repeating verbatim what they said, but about adding your own reflections to it. If you have any doubts, now is the time to frame them as clarifying questions and encourage them to tell you something more.

- **Always look for common ground.** If you're negotiating with someone, it's obvious that you two have different perspectives regarding the matter at hand. Even so, there's always something that can connect you to them—something that can be leveraged to build rapport with them. This is where your previous research about them comes in handy.

- **Ask open-ended questions throughout.** When we're invested in getting the other party to agree to our demands, we often focus on getting "yes" or "no" answers. However, these answers don't give us any clues about what the other party is thinking or what they truly want. For that, we have to rely on open-ended questions that encourage them to explore their own expectations and emotions as much as possible. For instance, instead of simply asking, "Can you give me what I need?" or even "Why can't you give me what I need?" try asking something like, "Could you tell me more about your apprehensions regarding my requests?" This simple reframing allows the other party to relax and talk about themselves rather than having to defend their position to you. Remember that close-ended questions aren't only those that result in "yes" or "no" answers but also those that keep the conversation from developing any further.

Framing Your Request and Crafting a Compelling Argument

In the first chapter, we talked about crafting a compelling value proposition statement for ourselves. In this section, we'll talk about what goes into preparing a compelling negotiation argument.

Structuring Your Negotiation Proposal

Here are a few things to keep in mind as you structure your negotiation proposal:

- **Make sure you've thoroughly done your research.** This point needs to be reiterated until we understand the importance of doing proper research. Good research will ensure that we're confident while asking for what we want, and it will also inspire respect and confidence in the other party.

- **Set a strong anchor.** What will be your initial demand? Is that demand justified? What is the basis for the demand, and can you provide evidence if asked? Remember that, as a woman, there's a chance you're already underestimating what you deserve. So, when deciding where to start, don't worry about how unreasonable the offer feels. Instead, try to find the logic behind your offer and work on communicating it with confidence.

- **Leverage data and examples to support your case.** The other party will likely have a difficult time understanding if your demand is legitimate, especially if they harbor an unconscious bias against women. At this point, data will be your best friend. Use industry benchmarks to support your case, ask for feedback and reviews to justify your worth, and highlight quantitative results wherever possible. For example, a mix of recommendations from your seniors and a snapshot of the growth your team has seen under you is a great way to convince someone to invest in you.

- **Explore options and trade-offs with the other party.** At this point, both you and the other party should know your highest and lowest limits, as well as your respective BATNA. What this means is that you can now reach a zone of possible agreement (ZOPA) with each other. Think of it this way: You need a minimum 20% salary hike but have asked for 25%. Your employer has told you they can only increase your salary by 15%, but in reality, they have the ability to go up to 20%. This means that you both have a "reservation point" of 20%. This reservation point is the point after which you cannot negotiate any further and must walk away. If you and the other party's reservation points are close enough to each other, you can reach a place where an agreement is possible. To reach there, however, you both will have to explore various options and trade-offs. For instance, you might agree to a 20% hike if you're also given the option of working from home twice a week, which allows you to spend more time with your family. Your organization might be willing to give you all of this if you agree to mentor one management trainee every quarter.

- **Be ready for counteroffers.** As mentioned in the last point, if you and the other party are in the ZOPA, you might both provide counteroffers to each other. While counteroffers indicate that an agreement is possible, it's important to not get carried away. Examine the counteroffer as closely as you would the original offer. If you feel like you need more information or even more time, ask for it. In the case of having to mentor one management trainee per quarter, for instance, you might want to accept because you like mentoring and you feel like you're getting the better end of the deal. At the same time, make sure that you have the time required to mentor these trainees and that your responsibilities don't get in the way of doing a good job. Sometimes, you might have to take a break to consider these counteroffers, which you should do rather than rush to a conclusion.

- **Document all important points of the meeting and schedule a follow-up.** It's very rare that a negotiation turns into a contractual agreement within one meeting. Many times, especially if both parties are already on familiar terms with each other, things are agreed upon verbally, which can lead to confusion later. Therefore, make it a point to document everything that is relevant to the agreement and plan with the other party for a follow-up. If your organization promises a 20% salary hike, request to see a formal statement from the HR department to confirm this. You also need to know when that salary hike comes into effect and if something else needs to be straightened out before things become final.

- **Ask for feedback where relevant.** It might not always be possible to get feedback from the other party, except maybe in the case of negotiating with your own organization, but you can ask your team members for their feedback on what you can do better. If you tend to get emotionally charged at certain points during negotiations, being aware of it can help you become more emotionally intelligent during the next negotiation. Similarly, if you struggle with timing during negotiations, you can work on it the next time you have to negotiate for something.

In this chapter, we've seen that negotiation is a skill that can be learned by anyone, irrespective of their gender. Also, women usually have more power during negotiations than they might believe, as they can be empathetic and active listeners. Before we move on to the next chapter, let's create a checklist that can help you before and during a negotiation.

Negotiation Preparation Checklist

Here is a list of steps you should take before and during a negotiation:

- Clearly define your negotiation goals.

- Assess the value you bring to the table and create a compelling value proposition statement.

- Research your organization, industry, and market conditions and standards.

- Explore and determine your BATNA.

- Know your reservation point.

- If possible, try to figure out the other party's BATNA and reservation point in advance.

- Anticipate potential objections and counteroffers.

- Prepare your negotiation strategy—keeping in mind your and the other party's style as well as the purpose of the negotiation.

- Practice your pitch and hone your communication skills.

- Be aware of the context of the negotiation, and don't forget timing and setting when asking for what you need.

- Build trust and rapport through empathy and active listening.

- Document every important aspect of the negotiation process.

- Schedule a follow-up and prepare yourself for any challenges or changes that might arise.

- Ask for feedback, advice, and support to become a better negotiator each day.

- Check in with yourself and manage your mindset to ensure you're not giving in to internalized bias or underestimating what you can achieve through negotiation.

In the next chapter, we'll explore all the different ways in which we can negotiate for holistic career growth.

4

Beyond Salary—Negotiating for Holistic Career Growth

"Life is change. Growth is optional. Choose wisely."
Karen Kaiser Clark

Since we live in a largely capitalistic society, it makes sense that money is a major concern when we think about jobs and even careers. At the same time, we know that money cannot guarantee fulfillment, especially after a certain point. Since women have to contend with a gender wage gap at work, most of our energy goes toward trying to close that gap. As important as this is, we owe it to ourselves to improve the overall quality of our lives and to ensure that our workplaces support our mental, physical, and emotional well-being. In this chapter, we'll work toward negotiating for holistic career growth.

Identifying Nonmonetary Aspects of Job Satisfaction

Before you decide to negotiate for other aspects of your career, it helps to make a list of what matters to you. Here are some examples of nonmonetary aspects of job satisfaction:

- **Professional development opportunities:** Does your current workplace support your career development? Are you able to think beyond your current role and imagine a road map for your career? Professional development opportunities can vary from skills training within the organization to certifications that help you diversify and try different things in your career.

- **Mentorship and sponsorship programs:** We've talked about the importance of both mentorship and sponsorship in Chapter 2. If your workplace has these programs, it means they are serious about helping you on your career path. They understand the unique challenges that women face in the corporate world and are willing to put time and resources toward helping them break the glass ceiling.

- **Job enrichment:** No matter how well-paid you are, you're bound to get bored and feel unmotivated if your role doesn't challenge you after a point. A challenging role isn't the same as a frustrating one; it pushes you to learn more and grow as a professional without feeling unsupported or disgruntled. Job enrichment can only happen when your manager or a senior in your organization understands your skills and potential and gives you the opportunity to enhance your current role. Job enrichment, when executed well, can pleasantly surprise you even as it demands more out of you.

- **Awards and recognitions:** Being recognized by our organization or industry isn't just a boost to your self-confidence; it also adds to your value proposition statement. A company that awards its employees at regular intervals conveys gratitude, appreciation, and respect.

- **Learning and growth:** Does your organization give you

opportunities to grow as a professional? Does it provide regular training sessions, connect you to other professionals in the industry, or help you explore your passions and interests as much as possible? A good learning environment will not only enable you to become better at your current job but will also help you explore other aspects of your career.

- **Work-life balance and flexibility:** These aspects have always been important, but they've become impossible to ignore in recent years. As the world begins to explore different ways of working and living, professionals want more balance and flexibility at work. This is especially true for women, as they are more likely to handle caregiving or homemaking responsibilities while also trying to do their best at work. When your organization gives you the flexibility to work from home or at your pace, or it helps you choose how you can best show up at work, it not only shows faith in you but also makes you feel valued.

- **Health and well-being programs:** When an organization invests in taking care of their employees' physical and mental health, it attracts and retains the best talent. This includes comprehensive health insurance programs, counseling sessions, and provision for mental health breaks if needed. Another aspect of employee well-being is creating a diverse and inclusive environment where neurodivergent employees are valued and supported and where people can talk about their mental health challenges without facing stigma.

- **Autonomy and empowerment:** When you feel like you have control over your own career, you're likely to stay in an organization for longer. When you feel like your voice matters and your opinion is valued by those around you, you'll be motivated to give your best at work.

Think about the aspects of your current role that contribute toward job satisfaction, and make a list of those aspects that leave much to be desired. If possible, create a priority list that tells you which aspects of your career to target first.

Negotiating for Work-Life Balance and Flexibility

When we have to ask for greater work-life balance and flexibility, we often feel guilty about doing so. After all, we're asking our manager and team members to make adjustments and support us for something that enhances our lives. This is why many of us hesitate to ask for these things, even if we know we deserve them. Here are a few tips that can help us become better at negotiating for them:

- **Prepare well before broaching the topic.** As always, the key to a successful negotiation lies in preparing well for it. Get a sense of your organization and its views on work-life balance. If there are precedents in the company for what you're about to ask, get more information on them. It can also help to gather some data on the impact of greater work-life balance on the productivity of employees and the results achieved by other organizations.

- **Know exactly what you need and why you need it.** If you desire to work from home most of the days, you should be able to articulate why that's important to you. Is it because you have young kids at home and it's difficult to arrange for daycare? Is it because you live far away from your workplace and waste a lot of time on the commute?

- **Choose the right time to negotiate.** When asking for greater work-life balance or flexibility, it's best if you can articulate your value to the organization. For example, if you've just received a great performance review, you can ask for more flexibility at work. Similarly, if you're beginning a new role at your organization, you can include work-life balance in your negotiations.

- **Advocate for your organization as much as for yourself.** Remember that women usually do very well while negotiating for others, so to relieve yourself of any pressure, frame your negotiations as a way to add more value to the organization. For example, what happens when you can work from home and take care of your children? You're able to better focus on work without worrying about them. What happens when you save on commuting time? You are less tired, can spend more time with your family, and can be more productive at work. When framing your ask, always think, *How does my organization benefit from this?*

- **Negotiate in person.** This might seem like a small thing, but negotiating in person—wherever possible—can add a lot to your strategy. For one, you can better gauge the energy of the situation and the person you're negotiating with. It also shows that you're willing to give these negotiations as much time and effort as they might take.

- **Get the support of someone who has done this before or who believes in you.** This is where having a sponsor can really help, as they can advocate for you and convince the relevant stakeholders that this is a move that benefits both parties. Even if you have all the necessary stats to back you up, a sponsor can add a lot of weight to your arguments.

- **Anticipate objections and be flexible.** Since this is a negotiation, be prepared for the fact that you might not get exactly what you want. If you want to work from home all the time, your manager might push back and say they can only offer it to you three days a week. If you think that four days a week is the least you can accept, you can ask them if working a few hours extra on the days you come in will help. This way, you might be able to get more done in the office and have more time to yourself at home, especially with a reduced workload on those days.

- **Get it in writing.** Since these stipulations might not be part of your official contract, you'll need to ensure that there's written evidence of whatever is agreed upon. This is helpful, especially if your manager or HR representative changes in the future.

- **Set a trial period and check in with your manager.** If this is the first time your manager is agreeing to such an arrangement, they'll likely need proof that it can work well. Therefore, ask your manager if you can test this arrangement for the next few weeks or even months if needed. During this time, ensure that you regularly check in with them and establish clear lines of communication at all times.

- **Document your achievements.** If working from home helped you beat deadlines or improve your productivity, make a note of them. Similarly, if you were able to come up with more creative solutions because you were better rested, let your manager know about it. When they can see exactly how these changes make you a better worker, they'll be more enthusiastic about going along with it.

Advocating for Special Roles and Leadership Opportunities

You want to take on leadership roles at work, or you want more challenging roles that satisfy you and also help you shine. However, you're not sure about how to negotiate for them. Here are a few steps that can help:

- **Know and communicate your value and potential.** As with any value proposition statement, ask yourself what role you're targeting and why. Why do you think you can make a great leader? What makes you a good fit for a particular role? What differentiates you from others who might be vying for the same role?

- **Make yourself visible to important stakeholders.** In order to convince your seniors that you can handle critical roles, show them you're capable of taking initiative and delivering results. For this, you will have to look out for projects that challenge you but are also doable. Ask for more responsibilities in your current role, look for ways to contribute more than you're mandated to, and don't hesitate to talk about these achievements with your manager and colleagues.

- **Ask for constructive feedback and use it to improve.** As an individual contributor, you can get away by focusing solely on your own performance, but a leader is responsible for other people's performances and well-being. This means they should invite and consider feedback from everyone, especially those who report to them. Get into the habit of asking for constructive feedback and implementing it on a regular basis.

- **Use performance reviews to advocate for yourself.** Women are usually not in the habit of asking for what they deserve, which is why you might second-guess yourself even if you know you're a good fit for the role you're targeting. Again, it will help if you frame your ask as a benefit to the organization. Think about a current problem that you can solve or a few ways in which you can help your organization as a leader.

- **Work on developing your personal brand.** Before you can ask for a more challenging role or a leadership position, you need to be seen as one by the people who matter. This can only happen when you develop your personal brand. What does your personal brand include? Your personality, strengths, achievements, and everything that makes you *you*. How do people refer to you in your absence? What qualities do they associate with you? Why should you work hard on developing your brand? Think of how any brand works. If you don't know a brand, you'll have to be convinced to give it a try, but if you are already a fan of the brand, you'll be the one willing to pay a premium for it. Similarly, if people know and love your brand, they will seek you out for leadership positions instead of having to be convinced to do so.

Negotiating for Benefits and Perks

As crucial as salary is when negotiating at work, there are other benefits and perks that can enhance our professional and personal well-being. These benefits ensure that women feel supported in the workplace, prepare for their lives ahead, and stay in the workforce for longer. Before we move on to negotiating for these perks, let's understand the advantages that they bring us.

There are various benefits that an organization can bestow on women, but some of the most common ones are: retirement benefits (like having our employer contribute to our retirement plan), comprehensive health insurance, maternity benefits (like paid maternity leave, childcare assistance, and day-care support), and support groups that help women share their experiences and find community in each other's presence.

The most important advantage of these benefits is increased financial security for women. When it comes to health insurance, both men and women are affected by lack of proper coverage. In many cases, this leads to them delaying treatment and being worse-off in the long run (Collins et al., 2023). In the case of women, there are various aspects of their health that are ignored or dismissed. For example, those who suffer from menstruation-related issues, such as endometriosis, might have to deal with the pain during work. Similarly, menopause is another stage that women go through without adequate support. A comprehensive health-care plan can ensure that women don't have to stress about their health and well-being all the time.

When it comes to retirement, women are often at a huge disadvantage. For one, women usually start at a lower wage than men, and this wage gap only increases over time. Since women usually live longer than men, they need to ensure that their retirement fund supports them for a longer period of time. In general, a woman's retirement fund is 44% lower in value than that of a man who retires at the same time (Dickler, 2023). Organizations can help improve this scenario by paying women fair wages and also increasing their contribution toward their retirement fund.

A woman who doesn't need to constantly worry about her health, future, and her family's—especially children's—well-being is much less likely to drop out of the workforce. In fact, she'll be able to perform better at work and give her best to an employer who makes her life easier and respects her needs. This is why these benefits are not just about doing what's right for women but also about doing good business. According to a study, when businesses provide benefits to women, such as assistance during maternity and fertility, they improve their own performance in the process. (*Could Female-Specific Benefits Bring Women Back to Work?*, 2022). Similarly, a McKinsey report found that providing benefits to women at work could add 12 trillion U.S. dollars to the global economy by 2025 (Woetzel et al., 2015). Therefore, we have to focus on the fact that we're negotiating for a win-win situation in this case as well.

How to Negotiate for Perks and Benefits

Here are a few things to keep in mind as you negotiate for your benefits and perks:

- **Do your research and know what you deserve.** The best way to determine if you can negotiate for certain perks is by assessing the state of your organization and industry. Also, there might be certain laws in your state that mandate your organization to provide you with particular benefits. The more thorough your research, the more compelling your negotiation pitch will be.

- **Leverage your value proposition statement.** If you're someone who has done a phenomenal job for the last few years, you can ask your employer to support you when your circumstances change.

For example, you can say, "These are my contributions toward the organization. I would love to keep contributing, and it will help if I can get more assistance as a first-time mom."

- **Time your negotiations well.** Remember that most—if not all—of these benefits will have to come out of the organization's budget, so timing is very important. Also, if you're joining a new organization, make sure that you've negotiated for everything before you sign the contract.

- **Reconsider how you look at your compensation package.** As we've discussed before, salary is very important when considering a job, promotion, or new role. At the same time, your compensation package can include a lot more details, such as the amount your employer will contribute toward your 401K or the stock options they might provide, especially if they're a startup. In some of these cases, your in-hand salary might be a bit lower, but you might end up either saving a lot for your future or becoming wealthier over time. Similarly, your organization might give you the option of opening a flexible spending account where you can park some of your pre-tax money for future childcare expenses.

- **Deal with resistance in an effective manner.** There are two main ways in which you can handle resistance during these negotiations. You can ask them to review your performance within a specified time period to assure them that their support will only encourage you to do your best. You can also meet them in the middle. For example, if your organization is paying you a lower salary than you expected, you can use it to your advantage and ask them to include better benefits to offset your loss. At all times, assert the fact that you deserve what you're asking for.

You don't want to come off as entitled when negotiating for these perks. Instead, communicate how these perks will help you stay with the organization and give them what they are looking for in an employee.

Before we move on to the next chapter, let's take a look at some interesting and relevant job benefits that you can negotiate for and even use as parameters for choosing the best organizations to work with.

List of Benefits to Negotiate For

Here are a few benefits to consider during negotiations:

- gym memberships or online fitness classes

- nutritional counseling and holistic wellness workshops, especially for pregnant women

- free or subsidized therapy sessions for better mental and emotional health

- regular, free health checkups and preventative care

- contraceptive health

- paid maternity leave

- childcare, eldercare, and dependent care assistance

- support groups for better mental health

- transportation stipend and services—especially when traveling at night or out of your base location

- supporting funds for higher education

- certifications and training—for both technical and soft skills

- tuition or course fee reimbursement for courses related to current or future roles

- sabbaticals for those who want to take a break, explore new things, or pursue higher education

- starting or supporting advocacy groups that help attract and retain more women in the workplace

- paid time-off

- flexible hours or work-from-home options

- stock options

- matching retirement savings

- signing bonus, especially if the candidate has multiple offers and the organization is very keen to recruit them

Exploring Job Benefits That Align With Our Values

In Chapter 1, we talked about the importance of determining our core values and career values. We also talked about how certain career values can change over time—like how we might become more focused on work-life balance after reaching a certain stage in life—while our core values remain the same—for example, honesty and respect will always be important to us no matter what. When we're exploring job benefits, it is useful to go back to this list of values we've created and use it to decide which benefits to negotiate for.

1. Make a list of the most important career values to you at this point. List them in decreasing order of priority in case you need to choose between two or more benefits during negotiations.

2. Revisit company culture if you're negotiating within your current organization, and learn about it if you're shifting to a new one. Remember that an organization's vision and mission statement are often conscious brand-building exercises, but it is through its perks and benefits that you can learn more about its culture. For example, an organization might *say* that they want to be part of their employees' growth and learning journey, but do they invest in training programs, certifications, and tuition reimbursements for them? Similarly, they might speak about the importance of mental health at work, but do they provide "mental health days" or free counseling sessions to their employees?

3. Acknowledge that you'll likely not receive all the benefits you seek in one role. Therefore, think about what is urgent and important for you to feel seen, respected, and supported at work. This will also depend on your current stage of life; for instance, if you are planning for a child in this year or the next, you should actively seek out and negotiate for maternity and postpartum benefits.

4. Remember that in some cases, it's also possible for your current organization to introduce a benefit for you if they don't already have it in place. If continuous learning is an important value to you, you can negotiate for it by clearly communicating the value you bring to the organization and the value such a program will bring to you.

5. Revisit your current list of career values before appraisals and job searches.

In the next chapter, we'll talk about the importance of setting boundaries and being assertive during difficult negotiations.

Reflect, Grow, and Inspire

"Women supporting women is the most powerful force for change in the world."
Ntozake Shange

I want to pause for a moment to remind you of the story I started this book with: I was at the end of my tether, and I felt like I'd lost both myself and my direction. But that was a huge turning point for me, and in the end, it changed my life for the better, bringing me, in an around-about way, several opportunities. I needed to reach the breaking point in order to have the experiences I was meant to have. It's how I found my path, and if you've also found yourself in a similar position, it's how you'll find yours. Every challenge we face is an opportunity to learn, and, ultimately, we can control our experience. We may not always be able to change our circumstances immediately, but we always have power—the power to leave the job, the power to pursue a different path, the power to change course... Whatever it is, we always have a choice.

I wanted to circle back to this because I think it's important to reflect on the moments that brought us here and work out what we can learn from them. Unlocking the secrets of negotiation is only part of what you're doing here; you're on a journey of growth, and your negotiation skills will help take you in the direction you're aiming for, but everything you learn from your experience is part of that. So I'd like to ask you to think about this now: Why is it that you came to be exploring negotiation techniques? Was there a catalyst moment that told you to do something differently? What can those things tell you about the path you need to take going forward?

The "She's Meant to Be" series came about because I wanted to inspire other women to step into their power and remind them that they are worthy of everything they want to achieve. I hope that by this stage in the book, you feel alive and ready to take charge of your life and your career development. While we're paused for reflection, I'd like to invite you to join me in inspiring even more readers—and you can do that really easily, simply by leaving a short review.

By leaving a review of this book on Amazon, you'll help other women find it easily, and if you're also willing to include a little of your own story, you'll inspire them to take action.

As a woman in the professional world, it's very easy to feel less than, and when you start to feel like that, it can be difficult to find the drive to make the changes you want to see. Simply by sharing our stories and helping each other find the resources we need, we can empower and inspire each other.

Thank you so much for your support. As I said in the introduction, I believe there's no greater gift we can give each other than helping to revitalize each other's imaginations and reminding each other that we're worthy of everything we desire.

Scan to leave a
review

PART 3:
STRATEGIZE AND ENGAGE

5

Difficult Conversations—Assertiveness and Boundary-Setting

"Daring to set boundaries is about having the courage to love ourselves, even when we risk disappointing others."
Brené Brown

When we talk about how gender bias affects women during negotiations and otherwise in the workplace, one of the biggest challenges we face is in setting and reinforcing healthy boundaries. Since women are so often penalized for being aggressive even when they're only being assertive, it can feel tricky to determine what to ignore and what to push back against. Add to that, women are often told that they're "taking things too seriously" or that they'll lose out if they're "so sensitive" in the workplace. Years and sometimes decades of having people around us routinely downplay our emotions and frustrations can make it seem easier to just go along with what people expect from us. Not only does this make us ineffective negotiators, but it also corrodes our sense of self-worth over time. In this chapter, we'll learn about recognizing various forms of discrimination within the workplace—especially those that are easier to miss or downplay—and their effects on our mental health and job satisfaction levels. We'll also discuss strategies to deal with these biases assertively and set healthy boundaries in a professional manner.

Recognizing and Addressing Subtle Forms of Discrimination in the Workplace

Gender bias—as well as other forms of bias—have always been a part of the workplace, but as the world around us becomes more conscious of them, they take different, and often subtle, forms. In the past, for example, someone might get away with publicly humiliating their female colleagues or making inappropriate jokes at their expense. Now, sexual harassment laws are not only strict but also enforceable, which likely means that those behaviors have reduced drastically. However, they could have been replaced by words and behaviors that are more difficult to pin down or notice but are just as hurtful as more blatant forms of discrimination.

In general, there are three main types of discrimination to look out for—verbal, behavioral, and environmental. Verbal discrimination means using words and language that are disrespectful to or patronizing of women. These comments can be obviously sexist, or they can feel innocuous on the surface while being harmful to the person being subjected to them. Behavioral signals are those that use certain symbols and actions to convey disrespect for women or other marginalized identities. Environmental discrimination is basically systemic sexism. For example, an organization where sexism is either promoted or not fought against enough, where senior leaders don't actively hire women for senior positions or act as mentors for those in junior positions, is an environmentally unfriendly place for most women.

These types of discrimination are known as microaggressions. As the name suggests, they are often difficult to spot because they are relatively "smaller" in nature, and in many cases, the recipient of these aggressions cannot even say whether they have been attacked or not. They know they feel uneasy or upset but cannot trace their anger, sadness, or anxiety to a particular source. That being said, microaggressions play a huge role in the mental health and confidence levels of women in the workplace. Therefore, before we can discuss ways to deal with these microaggressions, we need to learn to identify them in our workplace.

Identifying Microaggressions and Biased Language in the Workplace

For clearer comprehension, let's understand microaggressions in terms of the three main ways in which they manifest in the workplace—microinsults, microassaults, and microinvalidations.

Microinsults

Microinsults are usually subtle forms of verbal or nonverbal communication that demean a person's identity. In some cases, the aggressor is unaware of their biases, but in many cases, they know exactly what they're doing. Let's understand this with an example. Say a woman occupies a senior position in the company and leads a group of both men and women. If a man in the group says, "It's difficult for men these days because they don't enjoy any gender-based advantages; I wish everything was based on merit, just like the old days," that qualifies as a microinsult. On the surface, it might seem like a sensible thing to say; after all, who can argue that merit shouldn't be the basis of promotions and hiring? What this statement *implies*, however, is that men are being unfairly treated, women are not really capable of rising to senior leadership positions, and there's inherent merit in how people were traditionally hired. This last part is the most important. This statement is rooted in ignorance—either willful or otherwise—of traditional hiring and appraisal practices being sexist and unfair.

Another form of microinsult that can be even more confusing for the recipient is when it takes the form of backhanded compliments. For instance, if you lead a presentation for your team and it's received well, a colleague might come to you and say, "Wow, that was one of the most logical presentations I've seen by a woman." At this, you might hesitate and think, *Is he complimenting me for being different from other women, thus implying that most women are not capable of logical thinking?*

Microassaults

Microassaults are usually intentional and, very rarely, a result of ignorance. In other words, if a person uses microassaults toward someone else, they likely know that the other person is going to be hurt. Environmentally, a microassault can look like a workplace where sexist jokes are either encouraged or not taken seriously. If your team members regularly share memes that belittle women, you're going to feel upset and unsafe around them. Similarly, saying things like, "Women don't make good managers" or "Women don't have what it takes to make difficult decisions" undermines a woman's worth in the workplace and makes them doubt their own capabilities.

One form of microassaults is when women are expected to look and behave in certain ways in order to be accepted and taken seriously. For example, a woman might be constantly asked to "smile" or "look pleasant," while a man isn't bound by the same expectations. In fact, a man who is aggressive will be given a pass, while a woman who is even slightly assertive will be called "difficult to get along with." Similarly, women are often asked to wear heels and makeup in order to look presentable. So many women are asked, "Are you unwell?" if they decide to go without makeup one day at work.

Microinvalidations

As the name suggests, a microinvalidation is any kind of language or behavior that dismisses the marginalized person's experiences and challenges. For example, a woman who complains about harassment might be told that she does not know how to take a joke. A woman who points out all the ways in which her workplace isn't fair is told, "Look at how far you've made it here. Would that have been possible if this place wasn't fair to women?" When a woman talks about the issues she's facing, she's asked to "man up" because hers aren't real issues and she's letting other women down by making "mountains out of molehills." Basically, the issues that are important to women are made out to be nonissues by others around them.

All three types of microaggressions can occur together, and they can be either verbal or nonverbal in nature. It can often take a while for the recipient of these microaggressions to realize that they're being targeted. Unfortunately, by the time many of us become aware of them, they have impacted us in deep and harmful ways.

How to Identify Them?

If you're new to identifying microaggressions at work, here are a few things that can help:

- **Become aware of what happens around you.** You'll be surprised at what you can learn if you simply keep your eyes and ears open. As women, we're often so used to microaggressions that we think it's best to either ignore them or pretend they're not happening. Trust me, I get it; it gets tiring and disappointing very quickly, and it's not our fault for not wanting to engage with these issues. However, nothing will truly change until we allow ourselves to observe what's happening around us. Start slow and be mindful of any triggers you might have, but don't give in to the trap of becoming numb.

- **Always reflect on intent versus impact.** This goes hand-in-hand with the previous bit of advice. As important as it is to be conscious of people's behaviors and words, it's also vital that we don't misread their intentions. As we've discussed earlier, it is possible that, in some cases, microaggressions occur without the understanding of the "perpetrator." This doesn't mean that they're absolved of all responsibility, but it does mean that you can separate intent from impact and focus on the actions, words, and environmental aspects that can be changed.

- **Seek feedback from others.** Constructive feedback is great for many reasons. For one, it can help you recognize your own biases. Also, it can help you understand if what you're observing and feeling is shared by others, especially those who are less powerful than you.

- **Document incidents that you witness or experience firsthand.** This is always important in almost every context, but it becomes critically so in a scenario where you and others are routinely dismissed or ridiculed for calling out microaggressions. Keep a record of all these incidents in detail so that if you need to escalate matters within or even outside your organization in some cases, they'll come in handy.

- **Educate yourself and others.** The more you keep yourself updated on your and other people's rights and responsibilities, the better your chances are of identifying microaggressions and holding your own when someone tries to dismiss or gaslight you. When it comes to educating others, there's an important nuance to keep in mind. While you can certainly contribute toward improving the culture of your organization by leading education and sensitivity seminars, for instance, you don't need to do the work *for* those who need to educate and change themselves. That is just burdening yourself even further because of other people's lack of empathy or unwillingness to evolve.

Understanding the Impact of Microaggressions on Mental Health and Job Satisfaction

Here are a few ways in which microaggressions negatively affect women at the workplace:

- **Increased levels of stress, anxiety, and depression:** When women are regularly subjected to microaggressions, they feel unsafe and tired in the workplace. The cost of working in a hostile environment is often a decline in mental and emotional health.

- **Physical symptoms of stress and anger:** When we have to constantly deal with microaggressions, it affects our bodies. For one, our bodies store trauma even when we don't realize it. Anger, stress, and sadness all become part of our bodies, sometimes leading to psychosomatic illnesses. Thus, the pain in your chest could be because of constant stress, and your stomach ache could be a symptom of anxiety. If you've been feeling fatigued and cannot find a physical reason for it—after consulting with a doctor, of course—there's a chance that your emotions are contributing to your physical ailments.

- **Feelings of resentment, isolation, and frustration:** One of the major causes for burnout is feeling disconnected from the work we do and the people we work with. While only a mental health professional can accurately diagnose burnout in a person, there are some symptoms that indicate this condition. For instance, a woman who feels misunderstood, targeted, and isolated at work because of microaggressions will struggle to connect with her work and her colleagues. She might also have to routinely suppress her anger in order to get by at work, which can lead to frustration and resentment in the long run. We'll talk about burnout in greater detail soon.

- **Struggles related to low self-worth:** When we have to deal with microaggressions at our workplace, it begins to chip away at our self-worth and self-esteem. Not having people around who value or celebrate us is difficult enough, but having to deal with those who see us as inferior can make us question whether we deserve respect and empathy in the first place.

- **Impostor syndrome and internalized misogyny:** Perhaps the most insidious effect of microaggressions on our psyche is that we begin to either justify or believe them over time. For instance, if you keep hearing from people around you that "women aren't fit for leadership positions" without any arguments to the contrary, you'll likely start to see it as a fact. Similarly, if you're "praised" for not being like the average woman, you can internalize those biases because they keep you comfortable and make you feel included in male-dominated spaces.

- **The phenomenon of self-rejection:** Dealing with microaggressions on a regular basis makes us lose faith in ourselves and discourage ourselves from trying for things that might work out for us. In general, women have a tough time believing that they're good enough for things, while men are confident enough to try even for those things that they're not particularly qualified for. This is a direct result of women having to deal with biases on a regular basis.

Strategies for Addressing Biases and Microaggressions Assertively

Here are a few steps you can take to ensure you don't let microaggressions and biases get to you:

- **Acknowledge that you're being treated unfairly.** This can seem like a small step but is extremely vital to your "assertiveness" journey. You first need to convince yourself that you are indeed being treated with unkindness and unfairness. For this, journaling can be a good option. In this journal, you can write down an incident that made you feel unsafe or disrespected. Don't worry about whether you're overreacting or not; simply write down how that incident made you feel. Keep making a note of such incidents and try to find out if there's a pattern of certain behaviors or words from a specific person or group of people. Each time, focus on how those actions or words make you feel. Remember to make these notes when you still remember the details of these incidents but are no longer intensely triggered by them. This way, you'll be able to record things with more clarity.

- **Figure out how you normally react to these microaggressions and why.** Each of us has specific responses for times when we feel unsafe or upset. A microaggression is a threat, and our bodies might react with one of the following responses: fight, flight, freeze, faint, or fawn (also known as appease). Your body might react in different ways depending on the realities of the situation before you. For example, if the person trying to insult you is a junior or even a peer, you can push back more easily than when your manager tries to invalidate you or your work. Paying attention to these responses can help us determine if they're helpful to us in the long run and if we can do something about changing them. For instance, the next time someone verbally attacks you, you might realize you have a habit of appeasing them and decide not to do that anymore.

- **Find ways to assertively respond to the microaggressions.** The first thing to do is to figure out what's the most important microaggression that needs to be addressed currently. This will ensure that you're not feeling drained or overwhelmed at any point. Then, decide how you can respond to the microaggression without becoming consumed by anger or stress. Often, the simplest things make a lot more difference than we might think. When a colleague or even a senior tries to make a sexist joke, for instance, you can simply feign ignorance and ask them to explain the joke to you. When they have to break down the joke, they often either realize how offensive it is or they understand that they're being politely called out. Similarly, if someone keeps talking about how men are the ones being discriminated against at the workplace, ask them to provide evidence of their claims. You can even have some evidence of your own ready if you need to refer to it at the time. More often than not, simply shining a light on the other person's words and actions can reduce the impact of the microaggression to a large extent and maybe even prevent it in the future.

- **Involve HR and senior leadership if needed.** There will be cases where you won't be able to handle these microaggressions on your own. If the other person is amenable to having a conversation about their behaviors, you should try and talk to them first. If, however, they are dismissive or worse, if they try to blame you for being "too sensitive," you'll need to approach HR and trusted senior leaders to step in for you. At this time, your records of previous microaggressions will come in handy.

- **Support others who have been affected.** Usually, people who engage in microaggressions don't limit themselves to one person, unless they're doing so because of a personal vendetta. Also, it's vital to remember the intersectional nature of microaggressions. For example, a Black woman will likely face worse discrimination than white women. Similarly, a woman—or even a man—from a working-class background can be discriminated against in elitist spaces. Therefore, always look out for people who might be dealing with similar or even worse problems, and offer your support to them if you can. Often, having a support group for those dealing with microaggressions can offer a much-needed space for everyone to vent and feel seen.

- **Leverage your power to create a culture of inclusivity.** We often get caught up in our helplessness, especially if we've been subjected to microaggressions all our lives. Instead, try to focus on what you have, and you'll be surprised to find out that you have greater influence over these things than you thought. Think of it this way: A culture where microaggressions are encouraged or not taken seriously enough can make it difficult for you to negotiate by reducing your self-worth, but you *can* negotiate for a better culture and ensure that these microaggressions don't affect you and others any more. Look for ways to be part of the solution, like helping HR conduct sensitivity training at the workplace.

Saying "No" Gracefully and Assertively

Picture this: Alia is a great worker and is appreciated by seniors and other colleagues alike at her workplace. She enjoys her job and usually looks forward to it, even when there's extra workload at times. Lately, however, she has noticed a change. She feels unusually tired on most days, even when she's not working. She doesn't have as much enthusiasm for work as she used to, and there are days when she dreads going to work. This doesn't make sense to her because there's nothing to be afraid of or worried about at work. At the same time, she notices that she now feels pressured at even the slightest of challenges.

Things come to a head when she starts getting angry without reason and has a difficult time being empathetic toward her colleagues. She has always prided herself on being kind and compassionate, so she doesn't understand why she's getting triggered and behaving this way of late.

Alia might not know this yet, but all the signs point toward her being on the verge of burnout, if not in the throes of it. Burnout is becoming more common lately, or at the very least, people are becoming more aware of its causes and effects. According to the World Health Organization, "burnout" is now seen as a disease caused when workplace stress isn't managed properly and on time (Robinson, 2023). It's possible to experience burnout in our personal lives as well, but we'll keep the focus on workplace burnout for the purposes of this book.

What Are the Symptoms of Burnout?

The tricky thing about burnout is that it creeps up on us until we're already drowning. Therefore, being able to identify the symptoms of burnout beforehand can help us take note and ask for help before it's too late. Here are some of the symptoms to look out for:

- **Physical symptoms:** Our bodies often reveal what we refuse to pay attention to. If you've been facing persistent sleep issues, exhaustion, or other physical problems like headaches and gut issues, chances are, you're inching closer toward burnout. The important thing to remember is that you cannot come to this conclusion by yourself. Always consult with a doctor and get a full medical checkup to rule out any other reasons for your ailments.

- **Emotional and mental symptoms:** Burnout can sometimes feel similar to stress, but they're not the same. Chronic stress can lead to burnout but otherwise, stress can be resolved once its source is removed. Burnout, on the other hand, is more persistent and sinister. Someone on the verge of burning out might suffer from anxiety and, in some cases, depression. They might lose confidence in themselves and feel like they're a failure, even if their performance says otherwise. Of course, over time, this will affect their performance and might even become a self-fulfilling prophecy. Burnout can cause us to become cynical and detached. We might struggle to connect with others and find meaning in our work and life.

- **Behavioral symptoms:** When we're struggling with burnout, we might have difficulty taking care of ourselves or others. We might also avoid confrontation of any kind and shirk responsibilities, as they add to our anxiety. In some cases, people might also resort to substance abuse and other unhealthy mechanisms of coping with their situation. Ultimately, all of this leads to poor performance at work and the danger of souring long-cherished professional relationships.

Burnout is a serious condition that can be life-threatening if not treated on time. In extreme cases, people suffer from chronic depression and even suicidal thoughts due to burnout. Therefore, it's important to get help as soon as possible.

What Leads to Burnout?

In general, there are three main kinds of burnout: overload, under-challenged, and neglect. Let's discuss crucial aspects of these in some detail.

Overload Burnout

As the name suggests, this kind of burnout occurs when we either have too much work to do for a considerable period of time or when we have to deal with frequent unreasonable deadlines. In many cases, we might have to deal with a lot of work without getting enough time off to rest and recuperate. While too much work is a problem, so too is work that doesn't have clear deliverables or instructions. While some people thrive in unstructured spaces and like wresting some order from the chaos, they also need to know what their responsibilities are at any given time. Without clear deliverables, one person might end up shouldering too many responsibilities at work, eventually leading to burnout.

Under-challenged Burnout

The other factor that can cause burnout is feeling under-challenged at work. Being under-challenged doesn't always mean having a light workload, which might work for someone who is looking for more of a work-life balance at the time. What usually happens is that the person is both overworked and under-challenged, meaning they are taking on busy work that doesn't add value to their professional lives. Not only that, but feeling under-challenged is also linked to feeling underappreciated at work. After all, it conveys a lack of faith on your manager's end if they cannot trust you with challenging and meaningful work.

Neglect or Unfair Treatment Burnout

In the first part of this chapter, we've seen how unfair treatment in the form of microaggressions can affect the mental and emotional health of women. Additionally, when their concerns are invalidated or when they have no one to talk to about their issues, the feelings of isolation deepen. It's difficult to feel connected with your work or workplace when you feel like you don't belong there. You might also be in a situation where you're putting in the work and not being recognized or rewarded enough for it.

Apart from these factors, there's a very important factor that often gets overlooked: our own personality traits.

Our Own Personality Traits

Sometimes, our own personality contributes toward burnout. For example, we might be hyper-independent and find it difficult to ask for help from others, even when they're willing to support us. This means we usually take on a lot of work and end up feeling exhausted and, sometimes, even resentful toward others. We could also be perfectionists, meaning we cannot be satisfied with our achievements and cannot let go of things easily. What this also means is that nothing is ever "good enough," which then becomes *I'm never good enough*.

Constantly chasing perfection—an ideal that, by nature, is unachievable—can eventually lead to burnout.

Those of us who have difficulty yielding control also tend to suffer from burnout. When we feel like we have to handle everything ourselves, we don't allow ourselves the rest that we truly deserve. It's true that, in many cases, women have no choice but to stay in control of things so that they're not taken advantage of or undermined at work. However, this comes at a huge price. The other side of this is women who feel like they have no control over their work and life. When we feel helpless on a regular basis and believe that the course of our lives is being determined solely by external circumstances, we lose the will to persist and find meaning in our work and lives.

Why Is Boundary-Setting Important to Prevent Burnout?

Let's go back to Alia's story. When things get difficult, Alia realizes she needs help, but she doesn't even know what is wrong. Talking to a therapist helps her understand that she's struggling with setting healthy boundaries at work. Since she enjoys her work and workplace so much, she's never really felt the need to rest or to dial back her responsibilities. As an empathetic person who is looked up to by so many of her peers and juniors and relied on by her seniors, she's never learned to say "no." At best, saying "no" feels rude and unhelpful, and at worst, it feels arrogant. As well-intentioned as Alia is, her lack of healthy boundaries is causing her a lot of damage. What's more, it's turning her into someone she doesn't want to be.

Whether we're feeling overworked, under-challenged, or neglected, chances are, we're not conveying our boundaries to others or upholding them when needed. Women especially have a lot of difficulty enforcing boundaries at work because they don't want to come across as "snooty" or "difficult." Another interesting, if sobering, aspect of burnout is that it happens in stages. In its initial stages, it manifests in the form of more work and a kind of "doubling down" of harmful behaviors. For instance, a woman who is just starting to burn out will usually take on more responsibilities and try to "prove" herself to others. This only worsens the symptoms of burnout and leads to more problems down the road. Therefore, the sooner we embrace and communicate our boundaries to others, the easier it will be for us and those who matter to us.

How to Set Boundaries at Work to Avoid Overextension and Burnout

There are three main kinds of boundaries that are essential to set at work: physical, emotional, and mental. Your physical space needs to be respected, your feelings should be honored, and you should be treated with fairness at all times. Here are a few ways in which you can set and maintain boundaries at work:

- **Clearly communicate your needs and concerns.** Don't wait for someone else to ask you for what you want or to figure out if something's wrong. Instead, communicate what you want from a scenario as clearly and early as possible. This helps set expectations at the outset, leading to less confusion in the future.

- **Determine your working hours and stick to them as much as you can.** This can be tricky in the beginning, and there could be days when you'll need to work beyond these hours, but those days have to be few and far between. Not only should you stop physically working beyond these hours, but you should also ensure you're not mentally occupied with thoughts of work. This also includes telling your colleagues and seniors that you'll not be available for calls after a certain hour.

- **Prioritize and delegate tasks.** Make peace with the fact that you cannot do everything on your own, nor should you. Make a list of tasks that are urgent and important for you and the value those tasks bring to your career. Think about the tasks that can be handled well if delegated to others, and have faith in them to do what needs to be done.

- **Limit the number of channels you use to communicate at work.** These days, there are far too many channels of communication at work, and they can leave us feeling overwhelmed. Instead, figure out one or two channels where you can be reached and where you'll respond diligently. Explain to others that being available everywhere doesn't work for you and this way, you can be more productive and present.

- **Make time for rest and rejuvenation.** No matter how much you love your job, you need to take breaks in between to perform well for a long time. Take advantage of the paid time off available to you, or negotiate for one after you've completed a project successfully. Even at work, try to set aside one hour or so when you don't focus on work. It could be a work-free lunch or 15-minute coffee breaks throughout the day.

- **Keep checking in with yourself to understand how you're feeling.** If you feel overwhelmed or exhausted at any time, you can treat it as a sign to step back from whatever's going on and think of ways to prioritize yourself in the moment.

- **Learn to say "no."** If you're not used to saying "no" to others, this is the perfect time to start.

Saying "No": Techniques for Diplomatically Declining Requests and Opportunities

When we're setting and maintaining boundaries, we often focus on the other person's feelings and reactions, which is why many of us feel guilty about saying "no." This is especially true for those of us who are empathetic or are conditioned to prioritize others over themselves. This is why we need a change of perspective before we implement ways of saying "no" to others at work.

For me, the biggest change occurred when I realized that my boundaries didn't exist for others' sake but for mine. Similarly, saying "no" to others was simply saying "yes" to myself—my mental health, my happiness, and my productivity. I suggest you do the same for yourself. Make a list of the things you lose out on when you say "yes" to people without having the bandwidth for it. Then, make a list of all that you can do when you say "no." Even if it means that you have more time to do "nothing," you're engaging in a radical act of self-care.

Here are some tips that can help you say "no" gracefully and firmly:

- **Thank the person for the opportunity, even if you decline it.** Even if you're not able to accept an offer from someone, let them know how grateful you are for the fact that they thought of you for it. This way, the other person will feel respected and appreciated.

- **Be clear, concise, and honest at all times.** The more you hem and haw while saying "no," the more insincere you'll seem. Instead, be honest about your reasons for declining something, and explain yourself as clearly and concisely as you can. If your boss asks you to take on a project, for example, you can simply say, "Thank you for the opportunity, but I can only do a good job if I focus on one major project at a time. Therefore, I'll have to say 'no' to this until I'm done with the current project."

- **Be as polite as you can.** Sometimes, the idea of saying "no" is so anxiety-inducing to us that we adopt a harsher attitude than we need to. Understand that your "no" will be received with a lot more positivity if you're pleasant about it. This is the time to use your empathy as well. For instance, you can say something like, "I completely understand how important this is to you, and I'm honored you thought of me for this, but I don't want to take it on and then do an unsatisfactory job of it." Remember, you're saying no to the project, opportunity, or invitation—not to the person providing them to you.

- **Think of alternatives and compromises where possible.** A "no" doesn't have to be final. Think of what you can offer along with the "no." Can you refer them to someone you know would love taking on the project? Can you help them in exchange for their help on something else? Can you support them in other ways that don't take too much of your time and energy but are still useful to them?

- **Keep future possibilities open.** Unless you don't want to deal with the person at all, let them know that you are open to collaborations in the future. This way, you're only saying "no" to the present project and not to your professional relationship.

Managing Emotions and Maintaining Professionalism

Difficult conversations and stressful situations challenge our emotional stability and threaten to lead us toward unprofessional behavior. What we need to understand is that our emotions and concerns are valid, but how we deal with them is our responsibility. If we allow our emotions to get the better of us, not only are we conveying a lack of emotional intelligence to others, but we're also allowing those who undermine us to win. Therefore, let's look at a few ways in which we can become better at managing our emotions at work:

- **Label your emotions and observe them from a distance.** When we simply react to our emotions, we make impulsive decisions and behave in irrational ways that don't help us at all. Instead, learn to identify and label your emotions as they arise within you. For example, if someone is trying to belittle you in a meeting, tell yourself that you're feeling angry because of it. By simply doing this, you're creating psychological distance between you, the trigger, and the resulting emotion, making it easier for you to develop a measured response to it.

- **Take deep breaths whenever you feel triggered.** Deep breathing is also an effective way of bringing distance between your emotions and yourself. Apart from this, breathing signals to our brain that we're ready to switch from a fight-or-flight response to a rest-and-digest response. When we feel threatened, we're likely to react strongly, but when we breathe deeply for a few minutes, we're in a better position to deal with our emotions.

- **Take a break if you need to.** Remember that it's better to take a break and excuse yourself from a potentially triggering situation than it is to lose your cool and sabotage yourself.

- **Practice mindfulness throughout the day.** Mindfulness isn't a tactic to be used when you're upset as much as a practice to be followed at all times. There are three main components of mindfulness: staying in the present moment without giving in to either past or future concerns, observing our own emotions in a detached manner, and listening to what the other person is trying to communicate without attaching value or judgment to it. This can seem like an impossible task in the beginning, but consistent practice can help us make mindfulness a part of our lives.

- **Utilize the power of reframing your thoughts through affirmations.** When you feel your emotions getting the better of you, use affirmations to reframe how you think about the situation. For example, if you're anxious about your upcoming presentation and keep feeling like you're going to do a bad job, simply tell yourself, "It's okay to be a bit anxious, but I've prepared as well as I could, which means I'm going to present the best I can." You don't have to lie to yourself while using affirmations; instead, shift the narrative from an unnecessarily negative one to a more realistic one.

- **Visualize the worst-case scenario.** This point is related to the previous one. Usually, we react sharply to situations because we're worried about something bad happening. When we're able to mindfully visualize the worst that can happen to us in a scenario, we often see that there's less to be anxious about. On the other hand, seeing how negatively our reaction can affect our future can also give us much-needed pause before we react.

Before we move on to the next chapter, let's look at certain "assertive communication" scripts that you can build on in the future.

Sample Assertive Communication Scripts

Responding to Microaggressions

Script 1: "Hi, I've heard you call me 'logical' and 'rational' during our discussions, and while that sounds like a compliment—and you could have easily meant it as one—your tone is that of surprise, which indicates to me that you don't expect me to be logical for some reason. Since you use this term quite frequently, it feels condescending and patronizing. It would be great if you could respect my intellect without making me feel targeted."

Script 2: "I know you're used to cracking jokes in the team, and most of the team members enjoy them a lot. However, I know that I and other women don't appreciate them as they are sexist in nature. They make us feel unsafe and disrespected within the team, which affects morale as well as productivity. We would appreciate it if you didn't make these jokes in our presence."

Script 3: "I've previously discussed with you my concerns regarding the culture of this organization, but you always seem to downplay my concerns. It's possible that you have a different view than me when it comes to the culture here, but it makes me feel invalidated when you dismiss my experiences, which are shared by others. Also, saying things like 'We cannot possibly have a sexism issue because we have so many female employees' is neither helpful nor respectful."

Setting Strong Boundaries

Script 1: "I understand that many people in this organization work late, but that's not feasible for me as I like to go back home and spend time with my children. I'm also in favor of switching my mind off work once I reach home, as that helps me stay energized and give my best the next day. I'll certainly stay back if something urgent comes up, but otherwise, I would like to leave the office by 7 p.m. and stay off work calls at home."

Script 2: "I'm really honored you want me to helm a project as important as this, but I'm afraid my current responsibilities don't allow me to take it on and do justice to it. Of course, I'll be more than happy to do it if I can delegate some of my current tasks to my team members."

Script 3: "I would love to hang out with the whole team after work, but I've been working nonstop for the past week and I'm really looking forward to going home and resting tonight. I don't want to fall sick and make things difficult for everybody since we have another week to go before this project ends. Let's celebrate together then!"

In the next chapter, we'll explore the importance of collaborative negotiations.

6

Collaborative Negotiations—Building Win-Win Solutions

"Everything is negotiable. Whether or not the negotiation is easy is another thing."
Carrie Fisher

Negotiation is often a tricky thing to master because it seems steeped in paradoxes. On one hand, you need to be tactful and respectful during negotiations; on the other, you need to be straightforward and firm. Similarly, it's essential to be flexible and accommodating while also ensuring that your own goals are met. A negotiation should result in a win-win solution, but that solution should not feel like a huge compromise. It's understandably difficult, in the beginning at least, to recognize what a successful negotiation looks like.

There are two main types of negotiation: distributive and integrative. A distributive or win-lose negotiation is competitive in nature, where one party wins at the cost of the other. An integrative negotiation, or a win-win negotiation, is one where both parties work together to expand the pie so that each of them feels like they've gained something at the end. In this chapter, we'll understand the value of integrative or collaborative negotiations and also learn about the skills needed to become better collaborators during negotiations.

The Benefits of a Collaborative Approach and How to Adopt This Approach

Fostering Trust and Nurturing Long-Term Relationships

When we go for win-lose solutions during negotiations, we often win the battle but lose the war. In most scenarios, the party we're negotiating with is important to us beyond the issue we're currently dealing with. For example, if we're negotiating vendor terms with one of our partners, it's important to come to a solution that works for us today, but it's equally crucial that we maintain goodwill and nurture a healthy relationship with them over the long term. When the other party begins to see us as a reliable partner in their business, they'll be more willing to compromise and give us what we need from them.

There are two main ways to foster trust as a negotiator. The first thing to do is prove yourself to be trustworthy and fair. What does this entail? We need to be as transparent with the other party as possible. Of course, there will be certain aspects of the proposal that need to be kept to ourselves, but we can be honest about this as well. If we don't have sole decision-making capacity on a particular subject, we need to clearly communicate that to the other party. When setting terms for the negotiation, ask yourself if those terms are fair and whether you would accept those terms if you were in the other party's shoes.

The other thing to do is to show the other party that you're trying to make things better for both of you. Think of this negotiation as one aspect of your relationship with them. How can you derive mutual benefit through this and future negotiations? What can you offer them that will make them invest in this relationship? Are there any opportunities for future collaboration that can benefit both of you?

Achieving Mutually Beneficial Outcomes

Collaborative negotiation helps us achieve outcomes that benefit both parties. When the other party sees that you're trying to create value for both of you, they'll have greater faith in your future partnership. When creating your negotiation agreement, always think about what you can offer to the other party without feeling like you're giving up on something crucial to yourself or your organization. Always ensure that the terms of agreement are feasible for both parties and are sustainable as well. The negotiation might end then and there, but the relationship will only strengthen over time, so make sure all the terms make sense to both of you.

Strategies for Finding Common Ground and Creating Value

Here are a few tips that can help you create value during negotiations:

- **Pay attention to shared goals and interests.** Be clear about your own goals and interests before you start the negotiation. Learn about the other party's goals, interests, priorities, and concerns, and think about how the negotiation would help both parties achieve their goals. Since you're at the negotiating table already, remind yourself that you already have reasons to consider working with each other on the problem at hand. If you're trying to negotiate for higher pay, for example, it's because you want to feel motivated enough to stay in your organization and contribute toward its success. At the same time, your organization is keen on negotiating with you because one of its major goals is talent retention.

• **Capitalize on your differences.** As important as it is to highlight your shared interests, you also need to pay attention to your differences. One aspect of this is figuring out anything that might make this negotiation difficult or even unfeasible. Another aspect—one that often gets ignored—is to focus on how your differences can be beneficial to each other. For example, if you want your vendor to agree to your terms, think of what you have that they don't—like your brand value—and how you can leverage it to help your vendor in their business.

• **Use creative problem-solving to arrive at win-win solutions.** A lot of our negotiation preparation is done away from the other party, which makes sense. However, if you're keen on finding common ground and building a long-lasting relationship with the other party, you can involve them in finding solutions for certain aspects of your problems. One way of doing this is by looking for things to add to the pie that add lots of value to one party without making the other party feel like they've suffered a huge loss. For example, if you have some time in the week and you enjoy spending time around people with fresh energy, you can volunteer to be a mentor or trainer for a few hours each week. This way, you're providing your organization with a valuable service at no cost to you. This makes them even more interested in retaining you by agreeing to most—if not all—of your demands.

• **Build trust and rapport.** How do you move on from a transactional approach to a collaborative one? By building a rapport with the other party. For this, you need to conduct thorough research about them to know more about their concerns and to communicate effectively with them to prove that you have their interests in mind as well. We'll talk more about building rapport in the next section.

* **Maintain a positive attitude.** No matter how tough things get, if you are positive about the outcome, it often rubs off on the other party as well. When we're negotiating with someone, especially if it's for an extended period of time, we tend to mirror their attitudes. If you're combative or anxious, the other party will pick up on it and take a similar stance to protect themselves. However, if you are hopeful about arriving at a solution that works for both of you, they're more likely to mirror your positivity.

* **Keep contingency contracts in place.** No matter how confident you are about achieving your negotiation goal, it's always possible that things don't go your way. It's also possible that, despite your best efforts, you cannot reach a win-win solution. In such cases, you'll need to fall back on a plan B. Sometimes, this contingency plan can allow you and the other party to come to the best possible solution under the circumstances. While this can include some compromise for one party, it can also signal hope for future negotiations if the relationship stays intact.

The Role of Empathy and Perspective-Taking in Collaborative Negotiation

As long as we look at negotiations as a "us versus them" exercise, we'll struggle to create truly collaborative solutions. On the other hand, if we can put ourselves in the other party's position and understand their needs and concerns, we can build a rapport with them. When we focus on perspectives other than our own, we prevent ourselves from taking a narrow-minded view of things. Women are often conditioned to be more empathetic than men, mostly because they are prepared for caregiving roles at home and sometimes even at the workplace. Not only that, but women usually have to pay a higher price than men for their perceived lack of empathy. As is often the case, once a quality is deemed as "feminine," it becomes associated with "weakness." Therefore, an empathetic position is often seen as a vulnerable one, which is in direct contrast to the "cutthroat" world of negotiations.

The truth is more nuanced than that. Empathy is a much-needed quality in negotiations and leadership, which means that women might have more of an advantage than they think in such situations. However, what many empathetic people need to work on is setting and implementing boundaries and not letting their empathy get in the way of assertive communication. Let's discuss the important aspects of empathy in collaborative negotiation.

Building Rapport

The word "rapport" comes from the French word *rapporter*, which means to "bring back" or "carry something back." When it comes to relationships, "rapport" indicates how we relate to each other and how we reflect each other's energy and intentions. When two people share a rapport with each other, they are able to find commonalities that make them understand each other better, and they're also able to look past differences that could challenge the relationship. Sometimes, two people can effortlessly and instantaneously build a rapport with each other, while in other cases, it takes a bit of time and effort to do so. The good news, however, is that we can develop the skills needed to build rapport with the other party during negotiations.

Here are a few tips to help you do so:

- **Work on making a good first impression.** If you're negotiating with someone for the first time, first impressions matter. This includes your body language, punctuality, and confidence, but it also includes the amount of research you've done on them. The other party should know that you're interested in them as a potential partner, which means knowing enough about them to start the negotiations on the right foot.

- **Use positive nonverbal communication.** Nonverbal communication goes a long way in building rapport. Make sure your body language is open, not closed. For example, crossing your arms across your chest can convey an aggressive or inflexible stance, while a relaxed body posture indicates that you're comfortable in your current environment. Smile as often as you can, and maintain consistent but gentle eye contact with the other party. You don't need to stare at them or intimidate them in any way. Instead, mirror their eye contact patterns to let them know you're connecting with them.

- **Use their name.** This can seem like a small thing, but calling someone by their correct—and preferred—name can go a long way in building a connection with them. More importantly, failing to do so can put off the other person and make them feel as if you don't respect them enough to learn something basic about their identity. Referring to someone by name also signals that you've reached a level of comfort where you're both on equal footing with each other.

- **Look for ways to connect with them.** This is where your exhaustive research will come in handy. Once you find something that resonates with you, use it as an ice-breaker in your conversations. Small talk can only go so far when trying to build a rapport, so look for things that spark an interest in both of you. If you don't find something of interest through your research, ask them about their passions. If you find something commendable about them, compliment them for it. Just make sure that you're authentic at all times. Nothing is more off-putting than an insincere attempt at flattery or connection.

- **Mirror their behavior in a subtle manner.** When we observe the other person's body language and mannerisms and mirror them in a subtle manner, we convince them that we're just like them. It's easier to build a rapport with someone who already sees us as a team member. However, mirroring should be done tactfully because otherwise, it can seem like we're mimicking them or trying too hard to act like them.

- **Find the right balance between friendly and frank.** Contrary to popular belief, "brutal honesty" does more harm than good, especially if you're looking for a long-term connection. At the same time, someone who is candid without being cruel will often create a favorable impression on the other person. Our negotiating partners want to know that we're honest with them and also considerate of them. Being frank also implies that we don't want to dupe the other person to create favorable results for ourselves.

Understanding the Other Party's Needs

Since negotiation is ultimately about getting what we need, we can sometimes focus too much on conveying those needs to the other party. Don't get me wrong—it's absolutely essential to let the other person know what we need from them, but that is not the sole purpose of negotiations. When we're overly focused on our own needs, it shows in our body language and communication style. We might either talk too much, or we might only pretend to listen to the other person. We've all experienced presentations where our audience is merely nodding or pretending to follow along without actually paying attention to what we're trying to say. Sometimes, we can be guilty of becoming that kind of audience for the other party.

This kind of "passive" listening not only damages our relationship with the other party but also puts us at a disadvantage. When the other person is telling us something about themselves, they're offering clues that can be helpful while negotiating with them. Nothing is unnecessary; in fact, those bits of information that might seem superfluous are often more useful than you might think. Therefore, the trick lies not only in allowing someone to speak but in actually listening to them.

Active listening is a skill that takes some time to master, but once we do so, we can reap its benefits in every aspect of our lives. Here are the steps we need to take in order to understand what the other party truly needs from us:

- **Be mentally present when talking to them.** Mental presence is about more than avoiding distractions during your conversations with the other person. It also means that you're actively engaging with what they're telling you. Make a note of things you agree with, points you would like to add your own perspective to, and topics you would like clarity on. Even if you disagree with something, don't express displeasure or confusion immediately; rather, keep it as something to discuss once you've established common ground with them.

- **Be curious and interested.** While you shouldn't interrupt the other person while they're speaking, you should convey interest through your facial expressions and statements of acknowledgment wherever possible. Most importantly, express curiosity toward them and ask them as many questions as you can about their work. If you have established a certain kind of relationship, you can also move beyond work and ask them questions about other aspects of their life; just ensure that you're not overstepping your boundaries at any point.

- **Use open-ended questions to understand them better.** If you want to ensure that the person you're dealing with lets their guard down with you, open-ended questions are the way to go. These questions help you know more about the person without making them feel uncomfortable or targeted. Close-ended questions usually result in only "yes" and "no" types of answers, which means they don't encourage conversation. Open-ended questions are also a great way to handle potential conflict. If you disagree with the other person on a certain topic, instead of saying, "I don't think that's right," you can ask, "Why don't you tell me more about your position on this?"

- **Acknowledge and validate.** Your nonverbal expressions can certainly validate the other person's feelings and beliefs, and so can the act of paraphrasing. Once the other person is done speaking, you can paraphrase what they have said to convey your understanding and support. For example, if the other party is talking about their concerns regarding a future partnership between the two of you, you can start with, "So what I'm hearing is..." This is also a great time to talk about any questions you might have for them. Remember that acknowledgment is not agreement. What you're doing is letting them know that their feelings are valid, even if you don't share their concerns or emotions about something. This shows respect for the individual, despite any differences you might have with them.

- **Read between the lines.** The other person in the negotiation, no matter how comfortable they are with you, will likely keep things under wraps for the same reason as you. However, they can be conveying more than they intend to, and you can pick up on these cues if you listen carefully to them. What is left out is often as important as what is said, and their nonverbal expressions will help you pick up on them.

Before we move on to the next chapter, let's go through some real-life case studies that show us how we can build win-win solutions through collaborative negotiations.

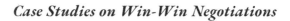

Case Studies on Win-Win Negotiations

Example 1: Negotiations between Volkswagen and the United Auto Workers (UAW).

The UAW is an American labor union that works for the interest of workers in the automobile industry. In 2013, automobile giant Volkswagen worked together with UAW to create a "works council" at one of their plants in Tennessee (*Collaboration: Collaborative Negotiation: Building Strong Partnerships*, 2024). A works council helps to represent and secure the economic and social rights of employees through its employers. As we can imagine, these negotiations can be tricky because each party has their own interests to defend. However, these negotiations were successful because both parties trusted each other and were willing to be flexible on certain points.

Insight/Takeaway: Without trust, negotiations are bound to fail, especially if you're looking to establish a long-term relationship. Ultimately, both parties need to come to a conclusion about their shared objectives and be flexible about what they can and cannot achieve through negotiations. When both parties are open to cooperation—even when they seem to be on opposite ends of a scenario—it leads to solutions that work for both of them. In this case, a well-established works council helps the employees believe that their rights are protected by the organization they work for, and it also helps the organization retain its best employees and gain a reputation as a fair employer in the market.

Example 2: Negotiations between New York City and Service Employees International Union (SEIU).

The SEIU is a labor organization that represents the interests of workers in over 100 occupations in the United States and Canada. In 2014, fast-food workers in New York decided to protest against the minimum hourly wage paid to them. At the time, it was $7.25, which was increased to $15 after successful negotiations between the city and SEIU (*Labor Unions: Collaborating With Labor Unions for Full Employment Success*, 2024). The increased hourly wage came at a greater cost to the city, but it resulted in a happier and more satisfied workforce, which also led to better service for the residents of the city.

Insight: Sometimes, it can take a while for a collaborative solution to be reached, and one party might have to be assertive about their wants so that the other party understands their needs. At the same time, a truly win-win solution is one where both parties can understand the long-term impacts of their decisions and work toward a mutually beneficial relationship. The city had the foresight to understand that overworked and underpaid frontline workers will ultimately result in disgruntled citizens and a labor crisis, and it worked with the fast-food workers to come up with a solution that made them feel fairly compensated.

Example 3: A history of negotiations between United Parcel Service (UPS) and the International Brotherhood of Teamsters (IBT).

In 2018, UPS and IBT—another major US labor organization—capitalized on a history of collaboration to negotiate an agreement that ensured enhanced job security, wage increases, and improved benefits for the workers (*Labor Unions: Collaborating With Labor Unions for Full Employment Success*, 2024). At the same time, the company committed to investing in better technologies so as to ensure productivity and improved working conditions for their workers.

Insight: This wasn't the first instance of collaboration between the two entities; in fact, they had built trust and collaboration over the years. This proves that having a win-win mindset paves the way for a strong relationship that can form the basis for further negotiations down the road. A labor organization that has faith in an employer works to provide suggestions that can benefit them as well as their employees, and it also acts as a reliable medium between the organization and its employees. A satisfied workforce doesn't just save the company lots of money in lost work hours, strikes, and disruptions but also contributes toward the company's long-term success.

Example 4: The unlikely partnership between Microsoft and Novell

In 2006, two rival technology companies reached an agreement that was considered almost impossible by people in the industry. Both companies competed with each other in providing various software and services to customers but eventually decided to come together to build and market certain solutions. Not only did this improve the "interoperability" between their products—meaning, it allowed the products to work together and communicate easily—but it also gave their customers more flexibility to choose between their products and services (*Microsoft and Novell Announce Broad Collaboration on Windows and Linux Interoperability and Support*, 2006).

Insight: It seems that competition is inherently opposed to collaboration, but there is scope for competitors to come together and create solutions that benefit both of them. In this scenario, both organizations understood that they could make use of each other's strengths and capabilities to provide better service for their customers, thus increasing their customer satisfaction and even enhancing their customer base in the long run. In an industry where cooperation isn't always the norm—especially when it comes to proprietary software—these organizations collaborated in novel and interesting ways. This is also a perfect example of "expanding the pie" and "creating value" rather than claiming value.

Now that we understand the importance of collaborative negotiations, let's discuss some common negotiation pitfalls that we should avoid.

7

Overcoming Negotiation Pitfalls—Avoiding Common Mistakes

"If you approach a negotiation thinking the other guy thinks like you, you are wrong. That's not empathy, that's a projection."

Chris Voss

Let's do a small exercise: Think about the first time you believed that you weren't good at negotiation or that you had certain innate qualities that made you a "poor negotiator." Chances are, you might not remember the exact event that triggered these feelings within you, but you can get a vague sense of what your life looked like then. One thing is for certain—no one thinks of themselves as being inherently "good" or "bad" at anything when they are children. In fact, children probably have unreasonable amounts of confidence when it comes to their abilities or their chances of succeeding at various things. This also means that, at some point, we begin to internalize the messages that we receive about ourselves and others.

When we have to start making decisions at every stage of our lives, it helps to have certain heuristic techniques to rely on. These techniques cut down our decision-making time and help us make "good enough choices" in our personal and professional lives. However, what they also do is put a lot of focus on our "subjective reality" instead of facts and objectivity. While it's true that our subjectivity colors almost every aspect of our lives, it shouldn't take away from us the ability to analyze the facts of a situation and make decisions based on them.

When our subjectivity colors our way of thinking about certain situations, it gives rise to cognitive biases, which ultimately lead to erroneous, hasty, or delayed decision-making. As women, we have often seen firsthand how other people's cognitive (and emotional) biases can come in the way of fair and effective decision-making. As negotiators, we have the opportunity to identify our own cognitive biases that could derail the negotiation process. In this chapter, we'll talk about identifying and overcoming these biases and also discuss techniques to handle potential challenges and impasses during negotiations.

Recognizing and Avoiding Common Cognitive Biases When Negotiating or Self-Advocating at Work

In this section, we'll discuss two important cognitive biases that can affect how we negotiate and examine ways to avoid them.

Anchoring Bias

Suppose you're shopping for groceries online, and you go to your favorite website because there's a sale going on. There, you see a particular item priced at $10 and discounted by 50%. Chances are, your mind fixates on the fact that you're getting a $10 item for $5, and you're happy at getting such a good deal. Since your mind is conditioned after seeing $10, you probably don't stop to consider whether the price was hiked up before offering the discount. It's possible that the particular item isn't worth more than $6, meaning you haven't gained as much as you think. Or, you might be paying $5 for an item that should not be priced higher than $4, meaning you're the one at a loss, but your mind is only considering things from the perspective of the initial number ($10) you can see.

The effect at play here is known as "anchoring bias." Our mind has a tendency to fixate on the first number mentioned in a negotiation and use that number to make decisions throughout the process. The interesting bit is that this number doesn't even need to be relevant to the discussion at hand, but it can still influence the decisions we make.

Why is anchoring bias so effective? During negotiations, both parties are operating with varying degrees of uncertainty, so our minds seek something to hold on to. This is why, the moment a specific piece of information becomes available to us, we latch on to it. It's not just the content of this information that affects us but also its tone. If the information presented seems positive to us, we feel confident during the rest of the negotiation process, whereas a negative piece of information can dampen our enthusiasm.

How to Avoid the Anchoring Bias During Negotiations

We've seen that a lack of information usually underlies anchoring bias. This means that if we prepare properly and do comprehensive research, we will be in a position to avoid this bias. Here are a few things to consider while negotiating in order to deal with the anchoring bias:

- **Know the context within which you're negotiating.** What does the market look like? If you're negotiating for a salary, you should have information on how much the other candidates at your level are receiving in the industry. Without this information, you might accept an offer, thinking you're getting paid fairly, when you're actually being lowballed by the other party.

- **Decide if you should make the first offer.** Usually, people believe that the party making the first offer is at an advantage because they set the tone and direction of the rest of the negotiation. This is not always the case. Making the first offer works when you are aware of the zone of possible agreement (ZOPA), meaning you have an idea of the range within which both of you can negotiate. At the same time, you need to know whether the other party is aware of the ZOPA. For example, do you know how high the organization is willing to go when they're offering you a salary, and also be sure about the minimum you can accept as a salary? If both parties know the ZOPA—as is the case when they are equipped with enough information and when they have a long-standing relationship—it doesn't really matter who makes the first offer. Similarly, if the other party has a stronger sense of the ZOPA, you won't be able to sway them by making the first offer. Therefore, you not only need to do your own research, but you should also have a good idea of how well-informed the other party is.

- **Be sure about your own worth.** You can counter the anchoring effect with confidence if you know how much you are worth. For instance, if an organization offers you a certain amount of salary, but you know you are worth more than that, you'll not be influenced by the initial offer.

- **Recognize the interplay between information and leverage.** Regardless of who drops the initial offer, you can gain an advantage simply by recognizing that the anchoring effect is in play. When evaluating an offer—either yours or the other party's—learn to identify two critical aspects of it: the information (which becomes the anchor) and the leverage. For instance, consider this statement: "I deserve a minimum salary of X, and I bring with me years of experience that will turn around the productivity of your marketing department." Here, the number X is both information and anchor, as it sets the tone for the rest of the negotiation. The fact that you have so many years of experience and you'll bring value to your organization is the leverage you have over the other party. In other words, you're communicating your value to them while promising them value in return. Your organization might counter with, "We can only offer you Y (Y being less than X), but we're giving you the chance to head a dynamic department in the most prestigious organization in the industry. Here, the information is Y, while the leverage is the company's standing in the industry. Recognizing the leverage you have over each other can help you make a decision without the influence of the anchoring effect.

- **Be sure to reject the anchor if it doesn't work for you.** A common mistake that people make when they have to counter an anchor is that they offer the counter-argument without rejecting the initial anchor. When we do this, that anchor remains relevant and can unconsciously affect the decisions made by both of you. For example, if Y as a salary is too low for you, you have to categorically state that this doesn't work for you, along with the reasons for your rejection. Then, re-anchor the negotiation with a new offer that makes sense to both of you.

- **Don't rush to a decision.** The anchoring effect can cause us to panic if we don't have enough information and confidence in our own worth. If you feel like the initial anchor is weighing down on you, ask the other party for some time to consider your options, do some more research, and come back to the negotiating table with new terms.

Framing Effect

Let's go back to the online grocery store and consider buying a packet of chips. You have two brands to choose from, but you've recently decided to eat healthy, so you want to choose the "least problematic" option while still satisfying your cravings. On one brand's package, it states: "Now with only 30% saturated fat!" On the other, it claims: "Your favorite brand has 70% less saturated fat than before!" Chances are, you'll choose the second brand instead of the first one because it's framed in a more attractive manner. It tells you that you are now consuming 70% less saturated fat than before, while the first one reminds you that you're *still* consuming 30% saturated fat.

The framing effect often plays an important role in negotiations because our decisions can be affected by how information is presented to us. The reason this effect is so powerful can be explained by two heuristics. Remember that heuristics are measures that help us quickly make decisions. One of them is the "availability heuristic," which implies that we make decisions based on information that we can easily retrieve. Therefore, when information is presented in a memorable manner, we don't forget it as quickly, and that becomes the basis for our decisions.

Another heuristic is the "affect heuristic," which implies that if a piece of information affects us on an emotional level, we are more likely to base our decisions on that. The "availability bias" can be best understood by seeing how advertisements are made to be as memorable as possible so that people can recall the ad and the brand associated with it while making their purchase decisions. The "affect bias" can be seen in instances where people—like politicians—use emotions to influence the public and to move away from fact-based discussions on their performance.

What makes something more memorable to us or affects us at a deeper level, you might wonder. The way our brains are wired, we feel our losses more severely than we appreciate our gains. This means that if something is framed as a loss, we are more likely to take action to avoid it than if it is framed as a gain. In the example of the two brands of chips, the loss is positive—consuming less saturated fats is healthy for us—while the gain is negative, so we choose the one that highlights the loss, even if both packets effectively show us the same information. Knowing what we do now, how can we avoid falling into the "framing effect" trap?

How to Avoid the Framing Effect Bias During Negotiations

Here are a few things to keep in mind to avoid falling into this trap during negotiations:

- **Be mindful of how you and the other party use language throughout the process.** Is the other party emphasizing the loss you will suffer if you don't choose their option? Are they trying to tug at your heartstrings while negotiating with you? For example, when you're involved in salary negotiations with your current employer, they might offer you much lower than you want but urge you to accept for the sake of loyalty.

- **Reframe the arguments in your own mind.** Once you recognize that the framing effect could be at play during a negotiation, reframe the arguments made by the other party to ensure that you're viewing them with an objective lens. For instance, is it worth it to let go of a salary hike to support your organization? If a new organization tells you that they are considering other candidates for your position and they are willing to accept a lower salary than the one you want, they're trying to use the "loss aversion bias" that you might have. Knowing this, can you objectively decide if you should accept the offer? Can you determine what the real loss is for you? Is it losing out on the job, or is it losing out on the salary hike that you deserve?

- **Negotiate for longer and gather as much information as you can.** The deeper your involvement in a negotiation is, the less likely you are to be swayed by the framing effect. For example, someone who has deeply researched the work that a politician has done in the past will not be influenced by them, no matter how emotional their speeches might be. Similarly, if you know that your organization has paid someone else at your level the amount you're asking for, you recognize that the "loyalty" bit is an emotional trick to retain you without paying what you're worth.

- **Be absolutely sure of your negotiation goals.** If you know exactly what you want out of the negotiation and why you deserve it, you're not going to be too worried about the framing effect. For example, no matter how many other candidates a potential company might be fielding, you know you deserve your salary and you won't accept anything less than that.

- **If you can, offer multiple, but still manageable, choices.** Keep in mind that you can still negotiate within the ZOPA. For example, if your organization is keen on retaining you but is offering you $10,000 less than the annual salary you're seeking, ask yourself if you can accept it for this year and ask for a higher raise from the second year onward. This way, you're showing your loyalty to them while also asking for fair compensation based on your skills. When the other party has more options but not so many that they get overwhelmed, they begin to see the negotiation in a positive, conciliatory light. They see you as someone who is keen to work with them, rather than someone with a "my way or the highway" approach.

- **Create a list of points that can be framed effectively on your end.** What are the different aspects of your agreement that can be framed in such a way that you get the results you need? For example, do you want to frame the negotiation as a *relationship-strengthening* one, where you use your existing relationship as leverage to get what you want? Do you want your customer to focus on the problem they have or on the solution you're offering them? Do you say, for instance, "If you don't work with us, you won't be able to get rid of this problem," or do you say, "We are committed to finding you a solution for this problem if we work together." You're essentially saying the same thing, but in the first statement, you're focusing on the other party's potential loss.

How to Avoid Making Assumptions About the Other Party's Interests and Motivations

We've learned a lot about the effect of bias on negotiations throughout this book. Our cognitive biases can often lead us to make assumptions about the other party, which not only undermines our negotiation strategy but also jeopardizes our relationship with them. These assumptions can be about the terms of agreement, the motivations of the other party, and the interest that they have in working with us. What happens, for instance, if you believe that an organization isn't particularly keen on working with you? You'll likely be more aggressive, or at the very least, less pleasant with them than you would if you knew they considered you an asset. As human beings, it's impossible to get rid of all our biases when dealing with others, but we can become more aware of them and try to reduce their influence while making decisions.

Here are a few tips to help you avoid making assumptions that can negatively impact your negotiation strategy:

- **Always test your assumptions and examine your biases.** One of the ways to do this is by carefully examining how you usually make decisions. Do you let certain cognitive biases get in the way? For example, do you place more importance on how things are said than what is being said? Has that led you to make certain erroneous decisions in the past? Do you take politeness for good intentions, or do you do more research and let the other person reveal their intentions to you?

- **Don't jump the gun during negotiations.** If you're someone who wants to end negotiations as soon as possible, you might not allow yourself enough time to properly assess the information you have at hand. Instead of rushing to conclusions about the other party and their terms of agreement, take some time to understand them and their intentions.

- **Use active questioning to your advantage.** When it comes to asking questions, it's important to maintain a balance between asking too few and too many of them. If you don't ask any questions, you might signal either a lack of interest or overconfidence to the other party. If you ask too many, you might come across as poorly researched or trying too hard to establish a connection. Therefore, spend some time researching your questions and figuring out if they're worth asking. Also, the kind of questions you ask matter. When you want to know more about the other party, keep your questions open-ended and allow them to speak. When you feel like they're hiding something from you, use probing questions to go deeper and get the insights you need. If you want further clarity on a topic, ask clarifying questions in a respectful manner. Make sure that your questions convey curiosity and not judgment.

- **Involve a third party if you need to.** It can often be challenging to identify our blind spots while making assumptions about the other party. If you can, always ask someone you trust to weigh in on those assumptions. They might be able to point out some of your biases at work and can even provide information that helps you see the other party in a different light.

- **Check your sources to avoid confirmation bias.** Confirmation bias occurs when we look for information that confirms what we already believe about someone or something. We might not even realize it, but we might be rejecting information that challenges our assumptions and gaining more information that supports our biases. Therefore, it's also important to pay attention to your sources of information. If you get your information from flawed sources or from only one source, bias is bound to creep in. Instead, look for multiple reliable sources and keep verifying the information you receive from them. When you have different sources to choose from, you're less likely to give too much weight to one of them. If you find something that contradicts your point of view, don't dismiss it; instead, look for more information to either support or reject your findings.

- **Use information-based bargaining.** Information-based bargaining emphasizes collecting as much data as possible on the other party—both before and during the negotiation process. This means letting the other party talk, listening to them keenly, and asking for more information wherever needed. When you feel that you're making too many assumptions about the other party, look for information gaps that you need to fill in order to counter the bias.

Navigating Impasses and Deadlocks

No matter how well-prepared you are for a negotiation or how interested both parties are in reaching a conclusion, there's always a chance that you'll reach an impasse during the process. This could be because you cannot come to a solution that works for both of you or because you've uncovered a detail that makes it impossible for the agreement to go through. Things can also change during the course of negotiations; for instance, things can become heated and both parties might be unwilling to work together anymore. Encountering an impasse can be very frustrating, especially if you've already invested a lot of time and effort into the process. Here are some techniques that can help you break through stalemates:

- **Reframe the problem.** We've talked about the "framing effect" that is present during negotiations. You might think that the problem statement is clear to both of you, but it's possible that you're both looking at it from different points of view, also known as "frames." Therefore, it can be very useful to revisit the problem and restate what it is. If you can, reframe the problem statement in such a way that it takes into account both parties' perspectives and needs.

- **Change the scope or timing of the negotiation.** An impasse can also occur because one or both parties are looking at the problem from a narrow perspective. Sometimes, widening the scope of the negotiation or even changing it completely can help resolve the deadlock. For instance, if it is absolutely not possible for your salary to be increased as much as you want, can you shift your focus to the benefits offered—which might be much easier to negotiate over? Similarly, if you find it difficult to come to a conclusion right now, can you revisit the negotiation at a later date, when both of you will have some time to think over the terms and do more research if needed?

- **Look for easy trade-offs.** What is easy for you to compromise on, and what is something the other party can give up without feeling like they've lost out on something important? If there's an impasse regarding one aspect of the negotiation, always look for something that can be given up on your end without you feeling the pinch. Use that compromise to make the other party feel like you're still committed to working toward a common solution.

- **Move away from emotional and subjective terms of the**

negotiation. An impasse can also occur when one or both parties get triggered or influenced by certain aspects of a negotiation. During such times, it's important to move the focus back to the facts at hand. It's easy to be at odds when the focus is on individual perspectives and much more difficult to argue over facts.

- **Focus on building rapport when you reach an impasse.** When you reach a stalemate with the other party, it's vital to signal to them that you are keen to nurture the relationship beyond this scenario. Therefore, if you find it difficult to reach beyond a certain stage in the negotiation process, spend some time building or strengthening your rapport with them.

- **Use a third party to help resolve the deadlock.** Sometimes, you might need a third person to step in and resolve the impasse. Ideally, this should be someone who is either trained in mediation or who has the ability to stay objective and keep the discussion on track. They should also be someone who is respected by both parties.

Knowing When to Walk Away From a Negotiation

The knowledge that you can walk away from a negotiation is an empowering one. It helps you assert yourself throughout the discussion and also keeps you from accepting terms that are damaging or even insulting to you. What you walk away from is also a clear signal regarding what you will not stand for, which helps establish your reputation in the organization or industry you work in. Take your time to figure out your "walkaway terms" much before the actual process starts so that you are not caught unawares during the negotiation. Your walkaway terms are unique to you, but there are a few common reasons that can apply to almost everyone:

- **You have reached your "walkaway point."** In a negotiation, the "walkaway point" indicates the minimum value that you can settle for and still consider the outcome a success. Beyond this point, it doesn't make sense for you to continue negotiating. If you need a minimum X% salary hike to continue working with your current organization, that becomes your walkaway point.

- **You and the other party have no overlapping interests in the form of ZOPA.** The ZOPA is formed when both parties are willing to compromise and their values are close to each other. If one party's highest value is far from another's lowest, there's no chance of reaching a mutually beneficial agreement.

- **There's been no progress in negotiations.** If you've reached a stalemate and there seems to be no way of breaking the deadlock, it's better to walk away from the negotiation than to waste more time and resources on it. As discussed earlier, you should first try to resolve the deadlock before you decide that it's not worth it to pursue the negotiation any further.

- **You have much better alternatives available.** Remember our discussion on BATNA? Your BATNA helps you negotiate better because it gives you certain alternatives to the result you're hoping to achieve in your negotiations. However, it might be possible that one or more of the alternatives available to you are so attractive that you don't need to continue your current negotiations. For instance, if you've been negotiating for a salary hike with your current organization and you suddenly receive an offer from an equally prestigious organization—offering you more money than what you're negotiating for and also giving you certain benefits that you don't enjoy currently—the offer will be too good to pass up, and your current negotiation will be moot.

- **The emotional costs of the current negotiation outweigh the potential benefits.** If the amount of money or resources being used to achieve a successful negotiation outweighs the potential gains in the future, it makes sense to walk away from it. This applies to intangible costs as well; for example, if the negotiation process is taking a toll on your mental and emotional health, you have to step back from it before you experience burnout.

- **The other party's demands are unethical or unreasonable.** Only you can decide whether something isn't ethical or reasonable for you to agree on. While legal issues are easier to understand, ethical issues are often less black-and-white. This is why you have to get in touch with your personal compass, which will help you navigate these issues and let you know what you are uncomfortable with.

- **It's just not a great fit.** Ultimately, negotiations are about the compatibility and chemistry you have with each other. If you and the other party are incompatible on a fundamental level—for example, if you don't align with their cultural values or if your ethical values don't match with theirs—it's a recipe for disaster in the long term. It might also be that everything looks great on paper, but your gut feels like something's off. Honor your instincts and walk away from the negotiation.

Before we move on to the next chapter, let's look at some exercises that can help us identify our negotiation blind spots and improve our strategy over time.

Negotiation Mistakes Self-Assessment

Let's go through a few online resources that can help us enhance our negotiation skills through various exercises. I'd also like to add a disclaimer here that I'm not connected to any of these organizations in a personal or professional capacity; these exercises have simply been helpful to many, and I would like to recommend them to you as well.

Negotiations Self-Assessment Inventory by Tero International

This is an exercise that helps us identify the behaviors that we exhibit most during negotiations and the influence they have on the result. First, we take an inventory of our negotiation skills by answering a few questions related to our behaviors during negotiations. Our scores on this test tell us two things: a) which behaviors we rely on the most, and b) how intense our reliance on each behavior is. The five different types of behaviors that are explored in this assessment are avoidance, aggression, accommodation, compromise, and collaboration. The exercise also helps us understand how each behavior might lead to a specific set of outcomes and when those behaviors might be appropriate.

Negotiation Exercises from RedRock Leadership

This organization put together three negotiation exercises that can help beginners learn and practice negotiation skills in a fun manner. The exercises are role-playing, looking for a win-win solution, and playing the two-dollar game. Role-playing is an exercise that helps a person figure out their weaknesses while negotiating. The second exercise helps individuals get into the habit of looking for win-win solutions during negotiations, while the third exercise is a game that helps participants hone their negotiation skills by following certain instructions throughout the game (Ruby, 2018).

Are You A Negotiation Ninja Quiz by Everywoman

This is a fun quiz containing nine questions, each of which presents a scenario and then offers three alternatives to choose from. Based on your answers, you'll either be declared a negotiation "ninja," "novice," or other terms that help you understand where you are on the journey and what your strengths and weaknesses are at the time. Not only that, but you can also access certain resources that will help you work on your negotiation skills.

When you do these exercises, remember to be honest with your answers. Don't fall into the trap of answering what you think you should as an ideal negotiator; that will not help you recognize your true blind spots and work on them.

In the next chapter, we will learn about the challenges of negotiating in a virtual world and discuss ways to adapt to remote and hybrid work cultures.

8

Negotiating in a Virtual World—Adapting to Remote and Hybrid Work

"Women need to shift from thinking 'I'm not ready to do that' to thinking 'I want to do that- and I'll learn by doing it.'"
Sheryl Sandberg

The pandemic brought with it a shift in not only our work culture but also in our understanding of work. For most of us, it was a challenge to shift to a remote or hybrid way of working for the first time. The lines between work and home became blurry, and those of us who were caregivers had to balance those responsibilities with the demands of work. Another challenge that many of us faced for the first time was learning to negotiate and communicate virtually. The challenges of conveying trust and working collaboratively are usually compounded when we are separated by screens.

Moreover, this period offered most of us, but especially women, a chance to reimagine work, communication, and negotiation for themselves. Perhaps for the first time, many women didn't have to choose between work and familial commitments. They realized that they could negotiate for work arrangements that benefited them without hampering their productivity. In other words, they were able to negotiate for win-win solutions with their organizations. As challenging as the period after the pandemic has been, it has also helped us reimagine what work and life can look like for us.

Throughout this book, we've tried to reframe intimidating scenarios into opportunities for growth. This chapter is no different. Here, we'll discuss the unique challenges of negotiating in a virtual environment and learn how to build trust and collaboration in such an environment. We'll also learn how to master virtual communication and negotiation in a rapidly changing work environment.

The Unique Challenges of Negotiating in a Virtual Environment

Anyone who has ever been a part of a virtual meeting on Zoom, Microsoft Teams, or any other platform will likely have experienced a mix of emotions and challenges. On one hand, it can be very convenient to connect to people around the world without having to leave home. On the other hand, you've likely experienced what is known as "Zoom fatigue" as a result of always being online and communicating with people virtually. Why does this happen? What are the challenges that an online environment brings to our work life? Let's go through a few of them:

- **Issues related to technology:** When we're in the midst of a meeting and the network at our home refuses to support us, it can lead to a lot of confusion and frustration. Unlike at work, where everyone is on the same network, there can be issues because of the different networks we are on. We might experience lag during the meeting, or we might go offline at the most inconvenient moments. Since we are conditioned to look for real-time responses when we're communicating during meetings, it can be unsettling to not get those responses when we want them.

- **Concerns related to security and privacy:** It's difficult to ensure privacy and security in a virtual environment, as some networks might be more secure than others. Also, we have to rely on the assurances of other people regarding the privacy measures at their homes. Often, there can be leaks and other issues simply because of carelessness at home. For companies that work with highly confidential information, it might be impractical to implement remote or hybrid work for most departments. During negotiations, such issues become even more pressing because we might be recorded without our knowledge, or our counterpart might have someone off-screen trying to dictate the course of the negotiation.

- **Lack of focus and confidence:** For many people, the technology takes some time to get used to. Even if we're used to communicating with others through these platforms, doing so for long hours each day can take a toll on us. At the same time, many of us might struggle to focus on the screen or pay attention to everything that's going on in front of us. In most meetings, we might have to focus on more than one person at a time, and there's no guarantee that everyone will be in a quiet and distraction-free environment. It can be overwhelming to process all kinds of information that we're faced with during virtual calls.

- **Lack of nonverbal cues during meetings:** Our brains rely a lot on the nonverbal cues we receive from others during conversations. This means that we get information from the body language of others, which is something that is not available to us in virtual environments. Sometimes, some people might need to switch off their cameras to ensure better audio quality, which means we're effectively talking to them as in a phone call. Even when someone's camera is on, we can only see them as a "floating or talking head," which doesn't give us a lot of information about their body language. Additionally, it's difficult to maintain real eye contact during such meetings because people might be placed differently on different screens, not to mention it can be unsettling for some people to stare at another person through a screen.

- **Difficulty building trust and rapport in virtual settings:** There are many reasons why this can be challenging in virtual environments. As we discussed earlier, the lack of reliable nonverbal cues can make it difficult to form a bond with other people online or even to convey trust and openness on our end. In these environments, nuance is also lost. For example, a simple email can come across as aggressive to a colleague just because they cannot look at you to confirm your tone and intent in real-time. Similarly, when the lines between work and home are blurred, we might bring a lot more of our home-related energy and frustrations to virtual meetings and conversations. For many people, the ability to spend time in the physical company of others is important to build rapport with them.

- **The possibility of encountering cultural and linguistic barriers:** While remote or hybrid work opens us up to the possibility of meeting people from different cultural and linguistic backgrounds—which is an education in itself—it can also lead to confusion and miscommunication in the process. It can be challenging to not let stereotypes dictate our interactions with people from backgrounds different from ours. It also happens that something innocuous in our culture can mean something very different in another culture. Therefore, we might commit some awful faux pas due to a lack of context and knowledge.

While these challenges are very real and can be intimidating, it's possible to overcome them and make the best of virtual negotiations.

Overcoming Technology and Communication Barriers in Virtual Negotiations

Before we discuss the "human" aspects of ensuring better communication during virtual negotiations, let's look at some technical and technological aspects to work on.

Overcoming Technical Difficulties and Ensuring Reliable Connectivity

Frequent technical difficulties in the middle of negotiations can lead to frustration on both ends. It can also reduce the impact of the negotiation and lead to unnecessary and unintended deadlocks. Therefore, ensuring reliable connectivity during these meetings should be of utmost priority. Here are a few ways you can do that:

- **Invest in good hardware and software.** When it comes to creating a setup that allows you to work remotely, it can feel a bit overwhelming, not to mention expensive. However, when you take a long-term view of things, you'll begin to see this as an important investment in your career. Budget a certain amount for office-related equipment and choose those with the best quality. Also, keep in mind your specific requirements so that you don't end up overspending on things that you don't need.

- **Use external microphones and headphones to enhance the audio quality.** We often underestimate the importance of high-quality audio during meetings. Instead of relying on the audio output of your device, it's a good idea to invest in good-quality headphones and microphones to enhance communication during meetings. If you're worried about potential chaos in your surroundings during important meetings, investing in noise-canceling headphones can be a good idea.

- **Use a wired connection whenever possible.** With the rise in availability and affordability of Wi-Fi connections in most places, it's become common to use Wi-Fi for video calls. However, if you can invest in a wired (ethernet) connection, you'll notice that there's less lag during video calls. This leads to fewer instances of garbled video and audio, and it also makes it easier to have conversations in real-time.

- **Be aware of and manage your bandwidth according to your requirements.** Bandwidth refers to your internet connection's capacity to transmit data. When it comes to video calls, there's a very large amount of data that is needed, which means that these calls consume a lot of bandwidth. There are many factors that determine the bandwidth requirements for your video calls, such as audio quality, latency or lag, screen sharing, data usage through numerous file transfers, video resolution (for example, when you require HD video calls), and video calls on mobile. The first step is to assess the bandwidth you do have for video calls. You can do this by calling a technician or by using various online tools that are available for this purpose. You can also determine your bandwidth requirements depending on the medium that you're using for these calls. If you have limited bandwidth, you might have to make certain choices—like changing your video call settings, managing your data usage, and ensuring you are on a stable network—to get the best video call quality despite your challenges.

- **Do a technical check beforehand.** Before you start your meetings, spend some time checking your equipment and network settings so that there are no surprises during the meeting. It's also a good idea to monitor and manage your settings on a regular basis.

- **Practice using your video conferencing tools.** We can avoid most of the problems we face during video calls by doing a practice run before the actual meeting. This will not only let you identify potential technical issues before the meeting, but it will also give you confidence in navigating your setup so that you don't panic in case of any glitches during the meeting.

- **Have a backup plan in place.** Sometimes, despite all our preparation, something can go wrong during crucial meetings. In such cases, you will benefit from having a solid backup plan in place. Do you have a spare laptop or desktop you can use, for example? Can you hop on to a reliable mobile hotspot if there are issues with your Wi-Fi connection? Can someone help you with their setup for an hour or so, in case something goes wrong with yours during the meeting? Having a backup plan in place not only gives you peace of mind but also conveys to your meeting partners that you are committed to having a glitch-free meeting.

Compensating for the Lack of Nonverbal Cues and In-Person Interaction

While it can be a bit tricky to deal with the lack of in-person interaction during virtual negotiations, there are certain techniques we can apply in order to compensate for it. Let's look at various aspects of the meetings and how we can work on them.

Visual Aspect

- **Choose video conferencing over audio-based or text-based communication.** While all forms of virtual communication are limited with respect to the amount and types of information they can convey, text-based and audio-based ones are usually more challenging than video-based communication platforms. Video calls can give us an opportunity to look at other people and take in information about their mental and physical state. Unless absolutely necessary, ensure that everyone has their cameras on and can see each other on their screens.

- **Be mindful of your background and appearance.** Just because you're participating in a meeting from home doesn't mean that you have to give up on a smart and professional appearance. As much as possible, dedicate a specific area for your office work and make sure that area looks professional. It's also important to ensure that your space is well-lit and can clearly be seen on camera. Similarly, invest in your appearance as you would if you were going to a physical office, not least because it can affect your mental state and subconsciously prepare you for the negotiation.

- **Use a large screen if you can, and encourage others to do the same.** The larger your screen, the more connected you'll feel to others during the negotiation. When you can see more of the other person, you feel more relaxed and get more important cues from them.

- **Maintain eye contact as much as possible.** While it's tricky to maintain eye contact even during video calls, you can practice with a team member to see where your natural eye level falls with respect to other people's screens. There are also certain software available that help you correct your gaze during virtual meetings. If you can hold gentle eye contact during virtual negotiations, you will inspire trust and build a rapport with the other person. If you're someone who gets uncomfortable looking into the camera for long periods of time, practice doing so with someone who makes you comfortable.

• **Make good use of visual aids to express yourself clearly.** To counter the confusion that might arise during video conferencing, make use of visual aids like presentations, graphs, and infographics. Share as much information as you can using these aids so that everyone has access to the same information and can process it as quickly and efficiently as possible.

Verbal Aspect

• **Set a clear agenda for the meeting.** Even before you start your discussions, make it clear to the other participants what you will be discussing and for how long. This sets expectations and helps ensure everyone is on the same page.

• **Use a moderator to ensure the session goes smoothly.** If there are too many people in the meeting and various points of discussion to go through, there's a chance that there will be a lot of "talking over each other" during the meeting. To counter this, you can appoint one or more moderators who will keep the discussion on track.

• **Be clear and concise during the meeting.** Preparing well in advance of the meeting will help us be clear and concise during the meeting. Also, you should time your speech during practice so that you don't take up too much of other people's time.

• **Use your active listening skills.** It can be difficult to remove distractions and focus on the person speaking during virtual negotiations, which is why your active listening skills can come in handy here. The same rules that apply during offline negotiations are valid here as well. Pay attention to the speaker, refrain from interrupting or judging them too quickly, and use summaries and reflective questions to clarify any points made by them.

- **Adjust your speaking style for virtual negotiations.** How we sound online can be very different from how we sound in person, and this is further complicated by the quality of our microphones and internet connections. Therefore, adjust your volume while speaking and ensure that you can be clearly heard by others. Also, ask a trusted team member to evaluate your pitch, tone, and speaking style to determine if you come across as aggressive or confrontational.

Nonverbal Aspect

- **Pay attention to other people's nonverbal cues.** It can take a while to get used to reading other people's faces to get clues about how they're feeling, but it can be done with some practice. Video calls can offer us opportunities to learn from the tone, facial expressions, and gestures of the people we're negotiating with. These nonverbal cues can also help us overcome certain cultural or linguistic barriers by helping us understand how the other person is truly feeling at a particular moment.

- **Express yourself clearly through nonverbal cues.** Be mindful of the messages you might be sending to others through your gestures during video calls. As you practice, ask your team members to give you feedback on how you come across to them.

Building Trust and Rapport in the Absence of In-Person Interaction

If you want to build trust and rapport during virtual negotiations, here are a few things to keep in mind:

- **Be clear about the negotiation's context.** The clearer you are about the context of the negotiation, the higher your chances of building trust with the other people involved in the process. Keep checking in with your counterparts to determine whether they are aware of the context at any given time, and make efforts to clarify anything that might have been misinterpreted by them.

- **Use icebreakers and quick conversations to help everyone feel at ease.** Often, virtual meetings can feel very agenda-driven and time-constrained—for valid reasons—but that takes away from the rapport-building time that we get during in-person negotiations. Therefore, setting aside some time to engage in meaningful small talk can help us feel connected to the people we're going to do business with.

- **Compensate for the lack of contextual cues during virtual meetings.** As we've discussed, virtual meetings are constrained by the lack of contextual cues. Therefore, wherever possible, provide relevant information about yourself, your team, and your expectations from the process. Similarly, if you feel like you need additional information from your counterpart—especially if they belong to a different culture—make it a point to do so as soon as possible.

- **Be responsive at all times.** Even if things get a bit tricky, be respectful to your counterpart during negotiations. Respond adequately to them by expressing appreciation when needed, providing constructive feedback, and asking open-ended questions where necessary. When they know that your full attention is on them, they'll automatically warm up to you. An effective way to show your responsiveness is by summarizing the other person's points at regular intervals.

- **Try to be as friendly and personal as you can.** Here, I don't mean that you need to dishonor your boundaries and divulge personal information in order to forge a connection with other people. What needs to be done is find a point of connection with them and show who you are as an individual. The important thing is to not be detached from the people you're negotiating with but to connect with them beyond the negotiation process. Think about some of the stories you can share about yourself, and encourage them to talk about themselves as well.

- **Use humor wherever possible.** Humor is a great way to defuse tension, especially in virtual settings. If you experience a glitch or if things are getting a bit overwhelming, take the lead in making light of these issues so they seem normal instead of insurmountable. No matter whether you're in an offline meeting or an online one, laughter has an uncanny ability to bring people together.

Techniques for Maintaining Visibility and Influence in a Remote Setting

If you're a remote or hybrid worker, you've likely experienced firsthand the challenges of being visible to your coworkers and seniors and of exerting influence during negotiations. You might have difficulty proving your worth where necessary, be passed over for important projects, and experience trouble bonding with your team members. However, a few techniques can help you stay on top of things:

- **Choose your channel of communication wisely, and use video whenever possible.** There are times when email communication might be more appropriate, and times when nothing except video communication will do. Knowing the pros and cons of different channels of communication will help you choose what works best in any given scenario. Of course, wherever possible, choose video calls to show your face and establish a deeper connection with your team.

- **Establish clear communication guidelines with your team.** Let your team know when and how often to connect with you, what to discuss on a regular basis, and how to reach you when they need to. This also means establishing clear boundaries that your team should honor. Let them know when you are available for calls and when you aren't. Remember that working remotely doesn't mean you have no control over your space and time.

- **Overcommunicate with your team.** Working remotely shouldn't mean you become invisible to your team. In fact, use it as an opportunity to overcommunicate with your team. Keep them updated about everything you're doing, including your achievements and challenges. Make it a point to provide them with enough information about your career and the progress you've been making. Provide additional context where you think it's needed. Of course, you don't need to bombard everyone with information each day, but make sure you're doing it on a regular basis. Don't forget that virtual communication can leave a lot of room for confusion and misinterpretation, so do your part in keeping a record of your work and intent, in case it is required at any point in the future.

- **Schedule regular check-ins with your team.** This includes the team you manage as well as your seniors in the organization. Take the initiative to set up meetings so that you can understand what is going well and what is not working at any given time. Also, if you're a manager, make sure to schedule one-on-one meetings with them on a regular basis. It's also a great idea to figure out a way for the team to get in touch quickly in case of a crisis or an urgent matter of discussion.

- **Schedule time for play and "water cooler talks."** Just because you don't physically share space with your team doesn't mean there is no scope for bonding with them. It's important to schedule time for connecting with each other and getting to know each other beyond work. Figure out things that are common among you and try to engage more in discussions around those things. Brainstorm games that you can play online or information you can share with each other about your own lives.

- **Create a plan to establish your virtual influence at work.** Just as we need sponsors and mentors at work, we also need to figure out key stakeholders who can vouch for our work and who we need to influence in order to forge ahead in our careers. Since the challenge is to establish your visibility to those who matter, you need to choose at least three people who can connect with you on a regular basis and keep track of your work and achievements over time. Once you've determined who those people are, figure out a "virtual influence" plan with them. Have discussions about what they need from you and how you can provide it to them, and revisit your plan often to see if it still works for you.

Before we move on to the last chapter, let's go through a checklist of strategies to overcome various virtual negotiation challenges.

Checklist to Excel at Virtual Negotiation

- **Use "rich" communication tools whenever you can.** In terms of trust- and rapport-building abilities, the best form of communication is in-person. When that is not possible, video becomes the next best option, followed by phone calls and then emails. Therefore, whenever possible, use video to establish trust, exchange nonverbal cues, and simulate the benefits of in-person interactions as closely as possible.

- **Prepare yourself and your team prior to the negotiations and implement timely checks for the technology being used.** Invest in the right kind of technology for the negotiations, and ensure that everyone on the team has access to them at the same time. Choose the right equipment, make sure you check your setup regularly, and have a backup ready in case the tech fails you during the meeting.

- **Make an effort to build trust and rapport in an online setting.** Engage in small talk and let the other party see you and bond with you beyond work, take a genuine interest in their life, and use active listening, empathy, and honest communication to build rapport in the absence of in-person interactions.

- **Take measures to enhance security and ensure privacy at all times.** Use secure and encrypted communication platforms at all times, and seek the help of your IT department if need be. Use confidentiality agreements to ensure everyone is on the same page regarding privacy and security. Lead by example and ensure that your team maintains high ethical standards while engaging in negotiations.

- **Be mindful of cultural differences and work on overcoming them as a team.** If you have to work with people from different cultural and linguistic backgrounds, take the time to learn about the dos and don'ts in their cultures so you don't accidentally commit any faux pas. Also, make an effort to remove jargon or complicated language from your communication, and keep checking in with them to ensure that your messages aren't "lost in translation."

In the last chapter, we will learn about using our negotiation skills to influence and empower others.

PART 4:
EMPOWER AND ELEVATE

9

Negotiating as a Leader—Influencing and Empowering Others

"To handle yourself, use your head; to handle others, use your heart."
Eleanor Roosevelt

If you've ever held a leadership position, you know how exhilarating and confusing it can be to shoulder the responsibilities that come with becoming a leader. Not to mention the different directions you might find yourself being pulled in—now that you have to work with people of different functions and temperaments, all while prioritizing the vision of the team and organization. Leadership can feel like a thankless job at times, which is why negotiation skills aren't always what comes to mind when we think of leaders. There are two reasons for this: One, traditional leadership models are authoritative in nature, which means "the leader commands and everyone else obeys them." This isn't really a model conducive to negotiation. Two, negotiating as a leader can be misinterpreted as "trying to appease everyone."

The truth, however, is that negotiation is an essential skill for anyone who wants to lead an organization. As the definition of leadership itself undergoes a much-needed change, win-win solutions might just be what leaders need to add value to their organizations. In this chapter, we'll understand the importance of negotiations in leadership and also discuss ways to ensure stakeholder buy-in through negotiations. Additionally, we will discuss ways to empower and mentor others to become powerful negotiators.

The Importance of Negotiation Skills for Effective Leadership

Why should one invest in negotiation skills as a leader? There are many benefits to it, such as:

- **Building strong relationships with the teams they work with:** We've seen throughout this book how negotiations are key to long-lasting and mutually beneficial professional relationships. As a leader, it's essential for us to nurture strong relationships with our teams, as we need to be able to rely on them at all times. Through negotiations, we convey to them that we want their needs to be met as much as we want our own visions fulfilled.

- **Managing conflicts and fostering agreement between members:** A leader has to work with a diverse team and sometimes has to manage cross-functional teams as well. As such, they are almost always dealing with conflict. Conflict isn't even a bad thing, as it can foster creative problem-solving and really bring the strengths of a diverse team to the fore, but it's the leader's responsibility to ensure that these conflicts are contributing positively to the team rather than disrupting it. Negotiation skills come in very handy here.

- **Advocating for their and others' careers:** An important role of a leader is to advocate for their team members wherever possible. Negotiation skills help them do so by determining the terms and conditions under which these team members receive promotions, raises, and other perks by the heads of the organization. These skills also help them identify the leverage they have when they are advocating for themselves or on behalf of others.

- **Maximizing value for the organization:** A leader adds value to the organization, but in such a way that keeps their external and internal stakeholders happy. For example, they will be focused on increasing company profits but will also need to ensure employee satisfaction. Similarly, they cannot sacrifice their partner relationships just to increase their yearly profit, as that would have a negative consequence on their business in the future. Negotiation skills ensure that win-win solutions are found by "increasing the pie" for everyone.

- **Preparing for the unexpected:** How can a leader prepare for business emergencies? How can they achieve business objectives during volatile times? Negotiation skills help them anticipate any problems they might face during business discussions, hold their own when they are pressured by their partners, competitors, or seniors, and be more flexible while making demands from others.

- **Empowering the teams they lead:** A leader who is good at negotiation can act as a great role model and also help their team members, making them confident negotiators in their own right. A team of people who can advocate for themselves and others are well on their path to becoming strong leaders of tomorrow.

Strategies for Influencing and Persuading Stakeholders Through Negotiation

A stakeholder is anyone who has an interest or stake in a particular project or in the organization. Such a person has needs and motivations of their own, and they align themselves with the person or organization that fulfills those needs. Your stakeholders play a vital role in determining your success as a leader. Let's discuss ways in which we can influence and persuade these stakeholders.

Understand Stakeholders' Needs and Motivations

The first step is to identify who your stakeholders are. Are they external stakeholders like your business partners or are they internal stakeholders like your employees? This can help you determine their level of involvement, the amount and types of information you can exchange with them, and their chances of already being aligned with your objectives. When you identify a stakeholder, research and make note of their priorities, objectives, and incentives. What do they want above everything else? Why would it serve them to work with you rather than against you? What can you offer them as motivation when trying to work with them?

Engage in Effective Communication and Relationship-Building

The base of a stakeholder relationship should be strong, especially if you're looking at a long-term relationship. The most important thing is to build rapport with your stakeholders. We've discussed rapport-building in great detail in Chapter 6. For a successful stakeholder relationship, we also need to establish credibility. A credible person is one who can be trusted, which means that they're honest. It also means they have the right qualifications and skills needed to do the job entrusted to them. Your credentials will help establish your credibility, but sometimes you might need recommendations from those within and outside the organization.

Make a list of the things your stakeholders should know and those that are on a need-to-know basis. Don't be dishonest, but don't give away leverage by revealing more than the other person does. Having a clear communication strategy and establishing boundaries at the outset helps all parties be on the same page. Encourage your stakeholders to ask questions, and use your questions to better understand them. When you're trying to frame problems, do so in a positive manner. At all times, make your stakeholders believe in your ability to provide solutions.

The most important thing to remember is that not all stakeholders have the same communication styles, even if they are on the same team. Therefore, you will need to tailor your communication strategy according to each member's needs and style.

Employ Strategic Negotiation Planning

As with any negotiation process, you need to spend a lot of time preparing before the meeting. Your research on your stakeholders and your understanding of the business needs should together inform your negotiation strategy. Start by ensuring that you and your stakeholders are on the same page regarding your vision. Whenever conflict arises, use it as an opportunity to understand what can be changed in your strategy and what needs to be doubled down on.

Wherever possible, seek alignment between their and your goals, needs, and methods. It can be unsettling to deal with conflict when you're trying to establish collaboration, which is why you have to dig deeper into the causes of the conflict. For example, if you are receiving pushback from your team members regarding a new employee-friendly policy you've helped introduce, try to understand the reasons behind their pushback. Similarly, if your external stakeholders are hesitant to invest in a new venture, spend time with them to uncover the real reasons behind their decision.

An important part of influencing stakeholders is managing their expectations from the beginning. This means being clear about what you can and cannot deliver and countering any misconceptions your stakeholders might have regarding the scope of the project. As a rule, it's better to "under-promise and over-deliver" than the other way around. Managing expectations is also important because many projects suffer from "scope creep," meaning they start out fine and then slowly begin to expand in scope, threatening to drain your time, energy, and resources over things that had not been decided in the first place. Therefore, checking in with your stakeholders and managing expectations is something that needs to be done throughout the project.

Leverage Time and Adaptability

Spending more time on the negotiating table is more advantageous to you than you might think. Of course, if you've already given too much of your time to something, you might need to consider if spending more time on it is useful for you or not. However, when you spend more time with your stakeholders, it usually results in a win-win solution for everyone involved. If you're engaged in conflict resolution with your stakeholders, you can think of taking a break from active negotiations for some time. At the same time, you should keep in touch with your stakeholders and use this time to understand them better. Over time, you might get closer to them simply by virtue of having spent meaningful time with them.

Crucially, your stakeholders might change from time to time, which means that a particularly difficult stakeholder might not remain in the team after some time. This can make your life considerably easier. Sometimes, simply being patient (if you can) can resolve many of the challenges you currently face with your stakeholders.

Adaptability is another great way to successfully influence your stakeholders. Show them that you are willing to meet them in the middle, and give them a few wins to show that you're serious about your commitment. However, if you are convinced of the value of certain strategies, you should not compromise on them. Similarly, if a certain strategy is related to your principles, you should not give up on it to appease your stakeholders.

Using Your Negotiation Skills to Manage Stakeholder Expectations

We've seen how important it is to manage stakeholder expectations as a leader. Here are a few steps to take in the process:

- **Frame your proposal in alignment with the objectives of the organization.** This will ensure that there are no discrepancies between your vision and that of your stakeholders. It also helps keep both internal and external stakeholders on the same page and gives them a common frame of reference if there is confusion in the future.

- **Create a priority list of stakeholders.** There will be situations where your stakeholders might be in conflict with each other or where their interests might clash. During these times, you'll have to choose to cater to one stakeholder over another. While you should not insult the other stakeholder, you will need to invest more in the one who is crucial to your project at the time.

- **Make strategic concessions where you can.** Don't just give away your leverage or provide concessions to your stakeholders, even if it doesn't cost you much. Instead, use it as a means to prove your commitment to your stakeholders and to build and maintain goodwill in your relationship with them.

Empowering and Mentoring Others in Negotiation

How do you, as a leader, empower your team members by helping them develop their negotiation skills? Here are a few ways in which you can do that:

- **Provide opportunities for your team members to lead negotiations every once in a while.** Look out for opportunities where some of your team members can practice their negotiation skills by taking the lead during discussions. Even if you cannot give them the entire responsibility for a negotiation, let them take the initiative on certain aspects of it.

- **Provide formal training to help build negotiation skills.** Having a good negotiation coach can make a lot of difference to a novice negotiator and can instill confidence in them as they step into a largely male-dominated world. Apart from this, if you feel that certain formal training can also help them gain more confidence in their area of expertise, help them receive it.

- **Encourage critical thinking in your team members.** When you engage in brainstorming sessions with your team and allow them to think critically through the problems in front of you, you help them form their own skills necessary to do well at negotiations in the future.

- **Use role-playing to help them learn negotiation skills.** Before they participate in real-life negotiations on a regular basis, help your team members get used to different scenarios they might encounter through role-playing sessions and simulations. Let them get a sense of the different roles they can play in a negotiation, the strengths they can bring to a negotiation, and the challenges they can anticipate during these times.

- **Provide timely feedback and encourage self-assessment and reflection.** As a leader, you can help your team members by offering them constructive feedback on their negotiation skills. At the same time, you can help them honestly assess their strengths and weaknesses by encouraging them to take part in self-assessments and spending some time reflecting on their skills.

- **Foster an environment of empowerment and self-advocacy in the organization.** If you want your team members to believe in themselves and become the best negotiators possible, you need to change things systemically. Exercise your influence to create an atmosphere where your team members learn to advocate for themselves and their skills and where they feel empowered enough to take the first step during negotiations. If they feel supported and embraced by people in the organization, they're less likely to be negatively impacted by the gender stereotypes they have to encounter elsewhere.

Before we end this chapter, let's go through a leadership negotiation scenario involving multiple stakeholders with competing interests.

Leadership Negotiation Scenario

Clara is a manager at a large bank headquartered in Chicago, Illinois. She has worked at this bank for 15 years, starting from her first role as a teller to her current position as a manager. She is not only an excellent performer but is also recognized as a great leader by the other members of the bank staff. Her seniors see her as someone who is eager to learn, adaptable to different situations, quick on her feet, and trustworthy.

Despite her accomplishments and the accolades she receives on a regular basis, Clara feels like something is missing in her professional career. One, she thinks that her lack of an MBA degree is keeping her from getting the promotion she deserves. Two, she thinks that this degree can help her learn leadership and management skills that she cannot learn on the job. Thus, she feels stagnant and anxious and is eager to take her career to the next level.

After doing her research, Clara comes across a part-time MBA program being offered at a university near her. The program seems to offer all that she is looking for, but it has two main issues: it is expensive, and the classes are held on Saturdays, which means they clash with her current work schedule at the bank. Clara is now faced with a dilemma. She knows this program is her path toward a more fulfilling professional life but is unsure of the way forward.

Stakeholders and Interests

These are the different stakeholders and their interests in the scenario.

- **Clara:** Clara is the one who wants to move on to the next stage of her learning journey. She wants professional development, work-life balance, financial stability, and a dynamic learning environment.

- **The university:** It aims to enroll well-qualified professionals into their courses so that it can earn good revenue and also enhance their reputation.

- **The bank's management:** They are keen on retaining talented and high-performing employees, developing the next generation of leaders, and ensuring that the bank's operations continue smoothly and efficiently.

- **The bank's staff:** These are the people who look up to Clara and depend on her guidance and leadership to perform well. If Clara is engaged during Saturdays, they might have difficulty handling their tasks with confidence.

Effective Leadership Strategies for Negotiation

In order to negotiate effectively with her current organization, there are a few steps that Clara needs to take. Let's go through them one by one.

Preparation

Here are a few things for Clara to do to prepare herself for the negotiation:

- **Identify her goals.** First, Clara needs to be sure that an MBA is the path forward for her. She needs to figure out her career goals and determine if an MBA is the best way to reach them.

- **Research as thoroughly as possible.** She needs to research her course, university, its fees, course requirements, and other relevant details that will help her make a decision and convince the other stakeholders as well.

- **Understand the different stakeholders and their interests.** While Clara will understandably be motivated to enhance her career, she also needs to ensure that her bank staff, as well as leadership, are not negatively impacted by her decision.

Once she has prepared herself for the negotiation, Clara now needs to have a discussion with her leadership team.

Framing the Conversation

At the negotiating table, Clara needs to frame the conversation in such a way that it feels like a win-win solution for everyone. On one hand, she has to be able to address any concerns the leadership might have about the cost of the program and her availability on Saturdays. On the other hand, she needs to convince the leadership that this degree will help her become a better leader and the skills she learns on the course will enhance the productivity of the bank as well.

Negotiation Tactics

- **Proposing win-win solutions:** Clara should consider a few options where her organization can support her financially. In return, she can commit to staying with the organization for at least a few years after her course is complete. Similarly, she can start a mentorship program within the organization after learning all she has to from her course.

- **Creating a flexible schedule that works for everyone:** While Clara won't be able to change the schedule of her classes, she can offer to make up for missed work during the week. She can also try to be available for her staff when she's not studying so that they can discuss their issues in detail with her.

Communication

In order for this arrangement to work, Clara needs to consistently and clearly communicate what can be expected from her. She has to be transparent about the amount of time she'll need to focus on her course and the amount of help she might need from others to do well. Once a schedule has been decided and classes have started, Clara needs to keep management updated about her course, her progress, and any challenges she might face during that time.

Collaboration

It's quite possible that some leaders and staff might be apprehensive about a reliable and high-performing employee and leader like Clara needing time away from work and possibly having difficulty dealing with the pressures of the added workload. It's her responsibility to come up with a plan to deal with her extra workload and to convince her leaders that she's up to the task. She can also create this plan with her manager, who can help her balance work and studies without getting overwhelmed.

Regular Follow-Up

Throughout her course, Clara needs to keep checking in with herself to see if she is performing well in her studies as well as at work. She also needs to discuss her progress with her manager and course correct if her studies are getting in the way of her duties. Regular constructive feedback will help her stay on track and confident about fulfilling her goals without compromising on the organization's needs.

Insight/Takeaway

When there are multiple stakeholders involved in a negotiation, it can feel intimidating to convince them all and achieve our goals through them. However, when we take the time to identify and understand each stakeholder, their interests and concerns, and the challenges they face, we can come up with a strategy that works for us as well as them.

Now that we've learned about negotiating as a leader, let's move on to the conclusion of the book.

Conclusion

"Each time a woman stands up for herself, without knowing it possibly, without claiming it, she stands up for all women."
Maya Angelou

Often, we go through life thinking less of ourselves because of how the world treats us. We begin to internalize harmful and prejudiced views about our talents, abilities, and strengths. So many of us have grown up internalizing these voices that we cannot distinguish between them and our own voice. Therefore, we sometimes need a kind and compassionate voice that helps us see ourselves clearly and confidently. This book was written with the aim of becoming that voice for readers like you.

By the end of this book, I hope you have realized that you have the choice, the capacity, and the opportunities to recognize your own worth, hone your negotiation skills, and advocate for your and others' success at the workplace. You don't need someone else's permission or approval to be successful on your own terms, nor do you need someone else to fight your battles for you. You have everything you need to succeed and to create a life that honors who you are.

Here are a few takeaways from the book that I hope will inform your negotiation and empowerment journey in the future:

- **You are inherently worthy, and recognizing your worth is the basis of successful negotiation.** In order to negotiate successfully, you need to recognize your worth and be able to communicate it effectively to others. This includes crafting a value proposition statement that outlines your strengths, achievements, and unique qualities.

- **Effective negotiation is a learnable skill that can be mastered through preparation, practice, and a strategic approach.** Contrary to popular belief, negotiation isn't a skill one is born with. The first step toward becoming a good negotiator is recognizing that one can learn these skills with practice and preparation.

- **Gender-based stereotypes pose great challenges to women in the workplace, but they can be overcome.** There are many kinds of gender-based stereotypes that can affect how women are treated in the workplace. What's more, being exposed to institutional misogyny can also lead to internalized misogyny, which can make it difficult for us to believe in ourselves. Being aware of these stereotypes is the first step toward overcoming them and becoming better negotiators.

- **Negotiation in the workplace goes beyond salary and helps us create the career of our dreams.** While salary is usually the most important factor during negotiations, there are other aspects of our work—such as career growth, perks, benefits, and so on—that can be part of negotiations. Knowing what matters to us in terms of our career and negotiating for it can help us create a career that we are proud of.

- **Having a strong support system is crucial to our success as negotiators.** Having mentors and sponsors ensures that we don't feel lonely on our negotiation journey. While mentors can help us recognize our strengths and give us much-needed guidance on our professional path, sponsors can advocate for us in front of senior leadership and help us overcome any challenges we might face in terms of career progression.

- **Negotiation is a lifelong journey of growth, learning, and empowerment.** A good negotiator is one who is curious and open to learning at all times. They recognize that they can always learn more, even from those who are just starting out on their journeys. As a negotiator, you have to not only empower yourself but also those around you. As a general rule, the longer you spend on the negotiating table, the better you become at negotiations.

The journey is worth it. Start by taking the first step and by having faith in your self-worth, and very soon you will be leading negotiations within and outside your workplace.

You now have the knowledge, tools, and strategies needed to transform your career and life through effective negotiation; you just need to put them into practice. Look around you and think of what your professional life is missing right now. Whether it's about asking for a well-deserved and long-overdue raise or about creating a more flexible work schedule for yourself, whether you want to give yourself a new challenge or you want to contribute more meaningfully toward the success of your organization, now is the time to step up and ask for what you deserve.

We're All Worthy

We're all meant to be so much more than what the world would like us to believe, and this is your chance to help other women realize that.

Simply by sharing your honest opinion of this book and a little about your own experience, you'll remind other women that they, too, are worthy, and you'll show them where they can find the support they need to become skilled negotiators, stepping into their power as confident professionals.

Thank you so much for your support. I wish you every success going forward.

Scan to leave a review

Complete the Series

Grab a copy of *She's Meant to Lead* and *She's Meant to Speak* to complement what you are about to learn within *She's Meant to Negotiate*! The collection can be read in any order that you see fit for your goals.

Scan for Book
Collection

References

Ajami, L. (2022, April 14). 7 examples of workplace microaggressions and how to steer clear. *Berlitz.* https://www.berlitz.com/blog/examples-microaggressions-workplace

Angelou, M. (n.d.). *Maya Angelou quotes.* Harper's BAZAAR. https://www.harpersbazaar.com/culture/features/a4056/empowering-female-quotes/

Bailey, E. (2023, May 5). *Aligning your career path with your core values: A guide to values-based career development.* LinkedIn. https://www.linkedin.com/pulse/aligning-your-career-path-core-values-elan-bailey

Baker, H. (n.d.). Quote. In Political, inspirational and famous negotiation quotes (2023). *KARRASS.* https://www.karrass.com/blog/thoughts-and-quotes-on-negotiation-2

BATNA: What it means and how to get the most out of negotiations. (2023, February 5). Santander Open Academy. https://www.santanderopenacademy.com/en/blog/batna-meaning.html

Bearman, S., Amrhein, M. (2016, July 8). *Why women hurt women: Understanding and overcoming internalized sexism.* Interchange Counseling Institute. http://www.interchangecounseling.com/blog/why-women-hurt-women-understanding-and-overcoming-internalized-sexism/

Brescoll, V. L. (2011). Who takes the floor and why. *Administrative Science Quarterly, 56*(4), 622–641. https://doi.org/10.1177/0001839212439994

Brinkley, S. (2023, June 24). *Four key approaches professional women can adopt to increase their visibility at work.* LinkedIn. https://www.linkedin.com/pulse/increaseyourglow-four-key-approaches-p rofessional-can-sheryl

Brown, B. (n.d.). Quote. In T. Gur (2023), *Daring to set boundaries is about having the courage to love ourselves, even when we risk disappointing others.* Elevate Society. https://elevatesociety.com/daring-to-set-boundaries-is/

Calero-Holmes, B. (2024, April 2). Essential negotiation tips to close the deal. *Business News Daily.* https://www.businessnewsdaily.com/7349-negotiating-donts.html

Caporuscio, J. C. (2020, July 22). *What to know about microaggressions in the workplace.* Medical News Today. https://www.medicalnewstoday.com/articles/microaggressions-in-the-work place#what-they-are

Castrillon, C. (2024, February 22). *10 ways to set boundaries at work to avoid burnout.* Corporate Escape Artist. https://corporateescapeartist.com/10-ways-to-set-boundaries-at-work-to-av oid-burnout/

Clark, K. K. (n.d.). *Karen Kaiser Clark quotes.* Goodreads. https://www.goodreads.com/quotes/143383-life-is-change-growth-is-optio nal-choose-wisely

Clarke, G. (2023, June 30). Aligning career & personal values: A guide for professionals. *Ginny Clarke.* https://www.ginnyclarke.com/blog/aligning-career-personal-values

A closer look at the professional development opportunities employees really want. (n.d.). *University of Massachusetts Global.* https://www.umassglobal.edu/news-and-events/blog/in-demand-professio nal-development-opportunities

CMA Consulting. (2023, October 19). *Mastering active listening skills: 15 essential tips for negotiation.* CMA Consulting. https://cmaconsulting.com.au/mastering-active-listening-skills-15-essential -tips-for-negotiation/

Coburn, C. (2020, December 14). *Knowing when it's time to walk-not talk.* Negotiation Experts. https://www.negotiations.com/articles/negotiate-when/

Cochran, S. (2024, March 18). *Non-monetary rewards to motivate your team.* E-Marketing Associates. https://www.e-marketingassociates.com/blog/non-monetary-rewards-to-motivate-your-team

Collaboration: Collaborative negotiation: Building strong partnerships. (2024, June 19). FasterCapital. https://fastercapital.com/content/Collaboration--Collaborative-Negotiation--Building-Strong-Partnerships.html

Collins, S. R., Roy, S., & Masitha, R. (2023, October 26). *Paying for it: How health care costs and medical debt are making Americans sicker and poorer.* The Commonwealth Fund. https://doi.org/10.26099/bf08-3735

A complete guide to BATNA, ZOPA & the reservation point. (2023, October 23). *KARRASS.* https://www.karrass.com/blog/batna

Connor, S. (n.d.). Influencing across distance: 3 strategies for impact. *IDEO.* https://www.ideou.com/blogs/inspiration/influencing-across-distance-3-strategies-for-impact

Cooks-Campbell, A. (2024, June 7). Signs of burnout at work — and what to do about it. *BetterUp.* https://www.betterup.com/blog/signs-of-burnout-at-work

Core values exercise. (n.d.). John Carroll University. http://webmedia.jcu.edu/advising/files/2016/02/Core-Values-Exercise.pdf

Could female-specific benefits bring women back to work? (2022, May 25). Kenan Institute of Private Enterprise. https://kenaninstitute.unc.edu/kenan-insight/could-female-specific-benefits-bring-women-back-to-work/

Cozma, I. (2023, October 23). Values, passion, or purpose — which should guide your career? *Harvard Business Review.* https://hbr.org/2023/10/values-passion-or-purpose-which-should-guide-your-career

Cuadra, D. (2022, July 15). Why sponsorship — not mentorship — may be the key to helping women advance their careers. *Employee Benefit News.* https://www.benefitnews.com/news/why-sponsorship-is-better-than-m entorship-in-womens-careers

Dalla-Camina, M. (2023, July 11). *Negotiating like a pro: The art of negotiation for women at work.* LinkedIn. https://www.linkedin.com/pulse/negotiating-like-pro-art-negotiation-women-work-megan-dalla-camina

Developing assertive communication as a woman in business. (2024, January 24). American Management Association. https://www.amanet.org/articles/developing-assertive-communication-as-a-woman-in-business/

Dickler, J. (2023, December 29). *Women are at greater risk in retirement. Here are ways to overcome a savings shortfall.* CNBC. https://www.cnbc.com/2023/12/29/women-face-a-retirement-savings-shortfall-three-ways-to-close-the-gap.html

Difficult conversations: How to control your emotions. (2022, July 28). Marlow. https://getmarlow.com/article/difficult-conversations-how-to-control-y our-emotions-1591915329950x806302991130296300

Doran, C., & Winkeler, M. (2018, January 8). *What is a BATNA, and how do I utilize my BATNA in a negotiation?* MWI. https://www.mwi.org/what-is-batna-in-negotiation/

Dussurgey, A. (2022, December 8). *The essential role of active listening in negotiation.* Sastrify. https://www.sastrify.com/blog/negotiations-active-listening

The Editorial Team. (2023, September 7). Top pay negotiation tips for women to earn higher salaries in 2023. *WomLEAD Magazine.* https://www.womleadmag.com/top-pay-negotiation-tips-for-women-to-earn-higher-salaries-in-2023/

Einig, S. E. (2021, February 24). *Building your personal value proposition.* LinkedIn.

https://www.linkedin.com/pulse/building-your-personal-value-propo sition-steve-einig

Ellevate. (2020, January 31). The anchoring effect in negotiation, and how to eliminate it. *Forbes.* https://www.forbes.com/sites/ellevate/2020/01/31/the-anchoring-effe ct-in-negotiation-and-how-to-eliminate-it/

Emerson, M. S. (2022, July 28). Women negotiation skills: How women can get what they want in a negotiation. *Harvard DCE.* https://professional.dce.harvard.edu/blog/women-negotiation-skills-h ow-women-can-get-what-they-want-in-a-negotiation/

Erkic, A. (2021, December 14).How to increase visibility at work as a remote worker. *Pumble.* https://pumble.com/blog/increase-visibility-at-work-as-a-remote-wor ker/

Examples of workplace microaggressions and how to reduce them. (2021, February 23). *Baker College.* https://www.baker.edu/about/get-to-know-us/blog/examples-of-work place-microaggressions-and-how-to-reduce-them/#microassaults

Ezell, D. (2023, April 5). The complete guide to remote communication. *TechSmith.* https://www.techsmith.com/blog/remote-communication-visuals/

Fann, R. (2024, January 16). Understanding stakeholder management: Guide for businesses. *Aloa Blog.* https://aloa.co/blog/understanding-stakeholder-management-guide-fo r-businesses

Fetti. (n.d.). *13 effective strategies to set boundaries at work.* Fetti. https://www.tryfetti.com/post/13-effective-strategies-to-set-boundarie s-at-work

Field, E., Krivkovich, A., Kügele, S., Robinson, N., & Yee, L. (2023, October 5). Women in the Workplace 2023. McKinsey & Company. https://www.mckinsey.com/featured-insights/diversity-and-inclusion/ women-in-the-workplace

Field Engineer. (2023, July 21). *The importance of work values: How they impact your career success.* Field Engineer. https://www.fieldengineer.com/article/importance-of-work-values/#how-to-identify-your-core-values

Fisher, C. (n.d.). *Carrie Fisher quotes.* Goodreads. https://www.goodreads.com/quotes/9325002-everything-is-negotiable-whether-or-not-the-negotiation-is-easy

Fisher-Yoshida, B. (2018, February 14). *How to correct implicit bias during negotiations.* Columbia School of Professional Studies. https://sps.columbia.edu/news/how-correct-implicit-bias-during-negotiations

Fonseca, N. (2021, September 13). *How to develop a growth mindset.* Great Place to Work. https://www.greatplacetowork.ca/en/articles/how-to-develop-a-growth-mindset

Fonseca, N. (2024, March 6). *4 easy steps to boost your mentorship program for women.* Great Place to Work. https://www.greatplacetowork.ca/en/articles/4-easy-steps-to-boost-your-mentorship-program-for-women

Framing. (n.d.). The Negotiation Challenge. https://students.thenegotiationchallenge.org/glossary/framing/

Fran. (2022, April 25). *What is a growth mindset and how can you develop one?* FutureLearn. https://www.futurelearn.com/info/blog/general/develop-growth-mindset

Furstenberg, D. V. (n.d.). *Diane Von Furstenberg quotes.* Goodreads. https://www.goodreads.com/quotes/278144-the-most-important-relationship-in-your-life-is-the-relationship

G, V. (2023, September 29). *Crafting your personal value statement: Examples to inspire success.* OnlineReputation.com. https://www.onlinereputation.com/personal-value-statement-examples/

Gaurav. (2023, February 7). How to set career goals that align with your values and aspirations. *Mentorrd.*

https://www.mentorrd.com/blog/how-to-set-career-goals-that-align-with-your-values-and-aspirations/?amp=1

Gibson, B. (2023, May 12). *What are the best negotiation strategies?*. Vistage. https://www.vistage.com/research-center/business-growth-strategy/six-successful-strategies-for-negotiation/

Gillham, R. (2022, September 24). Women salary negotiation (10 tips for 2022). *Blinkist   Magazine.* https://www.blinkist.com/magazine/posts/women-salary-negotiation-tips

Gittleson, W. (2024, February 12). *Procurement negotiation guide: Tips and resources.* Responsive. https://www.responsive.io/blog/procurement-negotiation/

Hailey, L. (2024, March 27). *20 ways to negotiate a salary after the job offer.* Science of People. https://www.scienceofpeople.com/ways-to-negotiate-salary/

Half, R. (2024, January 16). *10 negotiation skills for career advancement.* Robert   Half. https://www.roberthalf.com/us/en/insights/research/10-negotiation-skills-for-career-advancement

Hartley, M. (n.d.). *How to develop assertive body language.* Mary Hartley. https://maryhartley.com/how-to-develop-assertive-body-language/

Heiling, D. (2024, March 1). *How to set boundaries at work.* Intuit Credit Karma. https://www.creditkarma.com/income/i/how-to-set-boundaries-at-work

Hendricks, A. (2023, February 1). *How to manage stakeholder expectations.* Simply   Stakeholders. https://simplystakeholders.com/manage-stakeholder-expectations/#heading-2

Hoffman, S. (2022, March 16). *Career advancement for women through sponsors and mentors.* ACAMS Today. https://www.acamstoday.org/career-advancement-for-women-through-sponsors-and-mentors/

Hofmann, T. (2020, April 27). Negotiation 4.0: Virtual negotiations in the age of social distancing. *C4 Center for Negotiation.* https://negotiation-blog.eu/negotiation-4-0-virtual-negotiations-in-the-age-of-social-distancing/

Houghton, E. (2021, June 8). *How to align your career with your core values to be happier.* LinkedIn. https://www.linkedin.com/pulse/how-align-your-career-core-values-happier-elizabeth-houghton

How can you address microaggressions that perpetuate power dynamics? (2023, November 16). LinkedIn. https://www.linkedin.com/advice/0/how-can-you-address-microaggressions-perpetuate-power-xrrsc

How can you use active questioning to gather information in a negotiation? (2023, October 26). LinkedIn. https://www.linkedin.com/advice/1/how-can-you-use-active-questioning-gather-information

How do you test your assumptions before negotiating? (2023, May 5). LinkedIn. https://www.linkedin.com/advice/3/how-do-you-test-your-assumptions-before-negotiating

How do you use data and benchmarks to support your negotiation strategy? (2023, September 1). LinkedIn. https://www.linkedin.com/advice/1/how-do-you-use-data-benchmarks-support-your-negotiation

How to build rapport through virtual negotiations. (2020, October 7). *Negotiations Ninja.* https://negotiations.ninja/blog/how-to-build-rapport-through-virtual-negotiations/

How to do a comprehensive skills inventory. (2020, June 4). All Things Admin. https://www.allthingsadmin.com/skills-inventory/

Hutson, K. (2023, May 9). *Women in leadership: 5 strategies for advancing your career.* LinkedIn.

https://www.linkedin.com/pulse/women-leadership-5-strategies-advan
cing-your-career-kate-hutson

Hutto, C. (2023, May 11). *How to negotiate your job benefits: 10
conversation   example   scripts*.   *InHerSight*.
https://www.inhersight.com/blog/negotiating/how-negotiate-your-jo
b-benefits

The Ivey Academy. (2022, December 16). *Use collaborative negotiation to
build   trust   at   work*.   The   Ivey   Academy.
https://www.ivey.uwo.ca/academy/insights/2022/12/use-collaborative
-negotiation-to-build-trust-at-work/

J, N. (2023, October 19). *10 common cognitive biases in negotiation and
how   to   overcome   them*.   LinkedIn.
https://www.linkedin.com/pulse/10-common-cognitive-biases-negotia
tion-how-overcome-them-nancy-j

Jallais, C. (2019, February 6). *The influence of close relationships and
perspective taking in negotiation: An interview with professor Jimena
Ramirez*.   Icon.
https://icon.ieseg.fr/the-influence-of-close-relationships-and-perspecti
ve-taking-in-negotiation-an-interview-with-professor-jimena-ramirez/

Jones, T. (2023, April 16). *11 proven ways to build rapport in your
negotiations*.   thoughtLEADERS,   LLC.
https://www.thoughtleadersllc.com/2023/04/11-proven-ways-to-buil
d-rapport-in-your-negotiations/

Kat. (2022, June 28). *Negotiating a salary (and other benefits)*. Corporette.
https://corporette.com/negotiating-a-salary-and-other-benefits/

Kat. (2023, February 6). *Mentoring advice: How to be a
great mentee (and how to be a great mentor)*. Corporette.
https://corporette.com/mentoring-advice-for-women/

Kaufman, A. (2023, November 13). Empowering women in the
workplace: 5 negotiation strategies for career advancement. *Vaco*.
https://www.vaco.com/blog/empowering-women-5-workplace-negotia
tion-strategies/

Kaufman, J. (2020, April 11). *Ethernet is worth it for video calls.* Jeff Kaufman. https://www.jefftk.com/p/ethernet-is-worth-it-for-video-calls

Kitch, B. (2023, February 24). 10 tips for managing stakeholder expectations. *Mural.* https://www.mural.co/blog/manage-stakeholder-expectations

Kohlrusch, L. (2021, January 28). *Online negotiation: 13 tips how to successfully negotiate online.* PACTUM. https://pactum-advisory.de/en/online-negotiations-13-tips-how-to-successfully-negotiate-online/

Krastev, S. (n.d.). *Why do our decisions depend on how options are presented to us?* The Decision Lab. https://thedecisionlab.com/biases/framing-effect

Krbechek, A. S., & Tagle, A. (2022, December 21). *The right mentor can change your career. Here's how to find one.* NPR. https://www.npr.org/2019/10/25/773158390/how-to-find-a-mentor-and-make-it-work

Labor unions: Collaborating with labor unions for full employment success. (2024, June 9). FasterCapital. https://fastercapital.com/content/Labor-unions--Collaborating-with-Labor-Unions-for-Full-Employment-Success.html

Leonhardt, T. (2016, October 12). *4 signs it's time to walk away from a negotiation.* LinkedIn. https://www.linkedin.com/pulse/4-signs-its-time-walk-away-from-negotiation-ted-leonhardt

Lomri, G. (2023, December 5). *Embracing flexibility: Empowering women in the workplace through flexible work arrangements.* LinkedIn. https://www.linkedin.com/pulse/embracing-flexibility-empowering-women-workplace-through-lomri-kkcze

Luc, K. (2023, August 25). Microaggressions at work: Recognizing & overcoming our biases. *Culture Amp.* https://www.cultureamp.com/blog/microaggressions-at-work

Luna, K. (2023, August 4). *How to negotiate for more vacation time at work.* Going.

https://www.going.com/guides/how-to-negotiate-for-more-vacation-ti
me-at-work

Madigan, D. (2022, November 29). *Women and negotiation: You
can ask for more, and you should.* ABA Law Practice Today.
https://www.lawpracticetoday.org/article/women-negotiation-tips/

Malyk, M. (2023, February 21). Gender Microaggressions
at the workplace: A complete breakdown. *EasyLlama.*
https://www.easyllama.com/blog/gender-microaggressions/

Mannix, E. A. (2005, August 8). *Negotiating as a team.* HBS Working
Knowledge. https://hbswk.hbs.edu/archive/negotiating-as-a-team

Martin, S. (2022, September 15). *How boundaries can
prevent burnout.* The Better Boundaries Workbook.
https://betterboundariesworkbook.com/boundaries-prevent-burnout/

Martins, J. (2024, January 8). *Impostor syndrome: What it is and how to
overcome it.* Asana. https://asana.com/resources/impostor-syndrome

Maynes, A. (2023, December 20). Top 10 successful negotiation skills to
master. *Grand Canyon University.*
https://www.gcu.edu/blog/language-communication/top-negotiation-
skills

McCollum, J. (2024, July 17). *The double bind for women—Being a razor
blade and a cupcake.* SHRM.
https://www.shrm.org/topics-tools/news/inclusion-equity-diversity/vie
wpoint-the-double-bind-for-women-being-a-razor-blade-and-a-cupcake

McGill, J. (2021, December 31). *How to use walk
away negotiation tactic to your advantage.* LeadFuze.
https://www.leadfuze.com/walk-away-negotiation/

Mentorship and sponsorship: The power of female role models. (2023,
September 27). *City CV (UK).*
https://citycv.com/mentorship-and-sponsorship-the-power-of-female-r
ole-models/

*Microsoft and Novell announce broad collaboration on Windows and Linux
interoperability and support.* (2006, November 2). Microsoft.

https://news.microsoft.com/2006/11/02/microsoft-and-novell-annou
nce-broad-collaboration-on-windows-and-linux-interoperability-and-s
upport/

Mozahem, N. A., Masri, M. E. N. K. E., Najm, N. M., & Saleh, S. S. (2021). How gender differences in entitlement and apprehension manifest themselves in negotiation. *Group Decision and Negotiation*, *30*(3), 587–610. https://doi.org/10.1007/s10726-021-09724-3

Negotiation. (n.d.). Stanford University | VMware Women's Leadership Innovation Lab. https://womensleadership.stanford.edu/resources/voice-influence/neg otiation

Negotiation advice for women. (n.d.). Lean In. https://leanin.org/negotiation

Negotiations Self-Assessment inventory. (2014). Tero International, Inc. https://www.tero.com/pdfs/negassessment.pdf

Obama, M. (n.d.). Quote. In V. Bubna (2020), *"There is no limit to what we as women can accomplish" - Michelle Obama.* SheThePeople. https://www.shethepeople.tv/home-top-video/michelle-obama-empo wering-quotes-girls-women-can-accomplish/

O'Brien, J. (2021, January 30). *5 winning ways to build negotiation rapport.* Supply & Demand Chain Executive. https://www.sdcexec.com/sourcing-procurement/article/21207595/p ositive-purchasing-5-winning-ways-to-build-negotiation-rapport

Pathak, N. R. (2023, March 8). Breaking the glass ceiling: How mentorship and sponsorship can empower women leaders to reach new heights. *E T H R W o r l d . c o m .* https://hr.economictimes.indiatimes.com/news/workplace-4-0/diversi ty-and-inclusion/breaking-the-glass-ceiling-how-mentorship-and-spon sorship-can-empower-women-leaders-to-reach-new-heights/98485616

Phan, J. T. (2021, March 10). What's the right way to find a mentor? *Harvard Business Review.* https://hbr.org/2021/03/whats-the-right-way-to-find-a-mentor

Plata, T. (2022, April 14). *Work burnout signs: What to look for and what to do about it*. The Boston University. https://www.bu.edu/articles/2022/work-burnout-signs-symptoms/

PON Staff. (2024a, March 5). *10 Negotiation training skills every organization needs*. Program on Negotiation at Harvard Law School. https://www.pon.harvard.edu/daily/negotiation-training-daily/negotiation -training-skills/

PON Staff. (2024b, June 20). *Ask better negotiation questions*. Program on Negotiation at Harvard Law School. https://www.pon.harvard.edu/daily/negotiation-skills-daily/ask-better-ques tions-in-negotiation-nb/

Porter, R. (2024, March 7). 8 awesome women's professional networks. *Vault*. https://vault.com/blogs/networking/8-awesome-women-s-professional-net works

Powell, A. (2024, April 5). Remote collaboration: 6 key rules and best practices. *Everhour*. https://everhour.com/blog/remote-collaboration/#1_Over-communicate

PowerSpeaking Team. (2023, June 21). How to communicate your value: Strategies for women. *PowerSpeaking*. https://blog.powerspeaking.com/how-to-communicate-your-value-strategi es-for-women#ch2

Preparing questions to ask in negotiation: A definitive guide. (2023, April 4). The Maker Group. https://themakergroup.com/questions-to-ask-in-negotiation/

Principles and tactics of negotiation. (2007). *Journal of Oncology Practice, 3*(2), 102–105. https://doi.org/10.1200/jop.0726501

Purushothaman, D., Kolb, D. M., Bowles, H.R., & Purdie-Greenaway, V. (2022, January 14). Negotiating as a woman of color. *Harvard Business Review*. https://hbr.org/2022/01/negotiating-as-a-woman-of-color

Quiz: Are you a negotiation ninja? (n.d.). Everywoman. https://www.everywoman.com/my-development/quiz-are_you_a_negotiat ion_ninja/

Raeburn, A. (2024, February 9). *How (and when) to say no at work*. Asana. https://asana.com/resources/how-to-say-no-professionally

Rathburn, N. (n.d.). Quote. In K. Gospos (2022), *30 best inspirational quotes about female strength and empowerment (Plus images)*. LH AGENDA. https://lhagenda.com/resources/quotes/30-best-inspirational-quotes-wom en-plus-images/

Roberts, C. (2020, February 16). *How to set healthy boundaries at work to avoid burnout.* CNET. https://www.cnet.com/health/how-to-set-healthy-boundaries-at-work-to-avoid-burnout/

Robinson, B. (2023, February 7). New outlook on burnout for 2023: Limitations on what managers can do. *Forbes.* https://www.forbes.com/sites/bryanrobinson/2023/02/07/new-outlook-on-burnout-for-2023-limitations-on-what-managers-can-do/

Robinson, J. (2017, August 7). How to negotiate for better work-life balance. *Optimal Performance Strategies.* https://www.worktolive.info/blog/how-to-negotiate-for-better-work-life-b alance

The role of empathy in negotiation: Understanding the other side. (2024, April 8). FasterCapital. https://fastercapital.com/content/Empathy--The-Role-of-Empathy-in-Negotiation--Understanding-the-Other-Side.html

Roosevelt, E. (n.d.). *Eleanor Roosevelt quotes.* Goodreads. https://www.goodreads.com/quotes/142537-to-handle-yourself-use-your-head-to-handle-others-use

Ruby, J. (2018, June 30). *Negotiation exercises for improving team success.* RedRock Leadership. https://www.redrockleadership.com/negotiation-exercises-for-improving-t eam-success/

Russell, J. S., Pferdehirt, W. P., & Nelson, J. S. (2018, September 1). *Critical project management skill: Negotiation.* Pressbooks. https://wisc.pb.unizin.org/technicalpm/chapter/negotiation/

Sandberg, S. (n.d.). *Sheryl Sandberg quotes*. Goodreads. https://www.goodreads.com/quotes/925094-women-need-to-shift-from-t hinking-i-m-not-ready-to

Sheehan, H. (2023, July 6). How to professionally say no at work (+ examples). *Fellow.* https://fellow.app/blog/productivity/how-to-say-no-at-work/#assess

Shonk, K. (2019, November 4). *Online negotiation strategies: Email and videoconferencing*. Program on Negotiation at Harvard Law School. https://www.pon.harvard.edu/daily/negotiation-skills-daily/online-negotiat ion-strategies-email-and-videoconferencing/

Shonk, K. (2020, April 6). *Videoconferencing in business negotiation*. Program on Negotiation at Harvard Law School. https://www.pon.harvard.edu/daily/business-negotiations/videoconferenci ng-in-business-negotiation/

Shonk, K. (2021, April 5). *Methods of dispute resolution: Building trust in online mediation*. Program on Negotiation at Harvard Law School. https://www.pon.harvard.edu/daily/dispute-resolution/methods-of-disput e-resolution-building-trust-in-online-mediation/

Shonk, K. (2024a, May 10). *A negotiation preparation checklist*. Program on Negotiation at Harvard Law School. https://www.pon.harvard.edu/daily/negotiation-skills-daily/negotiation-pr eparation-checklist/

Shonk, K. (2024b, May 23). *Framing in negotiation*. Program on Negotiation at Harvard Law School. https://www.pon.harvard.edu/daily/business-negotiations/framing-in-neg otiation/

Shonk, K. (2024c, June 11). *Women and negotiation: Narrowing the gender gap in negotiation*. Program on Negotiation at Harvard Law School. https://www.pon.harvard.edu/daily/business-negotiations/women-and-ne gotiation-narrowing-the-gender-gap/

Shonk, K. (2024, June 13). *What is anchoring in negotiation?* Program on Negotiation at Harvard Law School.

https://www.pon.harvard.edu/daily/negotiation-skills-daily/what-is-anc
horing-in-negotiation/

Shonk, K. (2024d, June 18). *3 negotiation strategies for conflict resolution.*
Program on Negotiation at Harvard Law School.
https://www.pon.harvard.edu/daily/dispute-resolution/3-negotiation-s
trategies-for-conflict-resolution/

Shonk, K. (2024e, July 2). *Challenges facing women negotiators.* Program
on Negotiation at Harvard Law School.
https://www.pon.harvard.edu/daily/leadership-skills-daily/women-and-
negotiation-leveling-the-playing-field/

Simosko, N. (2016, October 7). *Saying yes to high visibility projects – five
steps to visible success.* LinkedIn.
https://www.linkedin.com/pulse/saying-yes-high-visibility-projects-five
-steps-visible-nina-simosko

Siocon, G. (2023, December 25). *16 benefits for female employees: Helpful
ways to support women in the workplace. Ongig Blog.*
https://blog.ongig.com/diversity-and-inclusion/16-benefits-for-female-
employees-helpful-ways-to-support-women-in-the-workplace/

6 ways to handle work pressure. (2024, June 28). *Integrity Staffing Solutions.*
https://www.integritystaffing.com/blog/6-ways-to-handle-work-pressu
re/

Skills assessment worksheet. (n.d.). Community College of Vermont.
https://ccv.edu/documents/2013/11/skills-inventory-worksheet.pdf/

Spangler, B. (2003, November). *Reframing.* Beyond Intractability.
https://www.beyondintractability.org/essay/joint_reframing

Stakeholder management: 4 strategies proven to work. (2023, October 27).
Wrike.
https://www.wrike.com/blog/4-strategies-dealing-difficult-stakeholders
/

Team DigitalDefynd. (2024, April 10). *How can women
negotiate a better salary at the workplace?* DigitalDefynd.
https://digitaldefynd.com/IQ/women-salary-negotiation/

10 ways to support women in the workplace. (2023, November 30). *INTOO US.* https://www.intoo.com/us/blog/supporting-women-in-the-workplace/

Udealor, M. (2021, August 1). *Creating value in negotiation.* LinkedIn. https://www.linkedin.com/pulse/creating-value-negotiation-michael-udea lor

Using BATNA to gain leverage in a deal. (2019, June 5). Summit Advisory. https://summitadvisory.com/leverage-matters/

Values clarification. (n.d.). Zencare. https://zencare.co/mental-health/values-clarification

Venter, D. (n.d.). *BATNA explained.* Negotiation Academy. https://www.negotiationtraining.com.au/articles/next-best-option/

Vinney, C. (2020, February 13). *What's the difference between eudaimonic and hedonic happiness?* ThoughtCo. https://www.thoughtco.com/eudaimonic-and-hedonic-happiness-478375 0

Voss, C. (n.d.). *Chris Voss quotes.* Goodreads. https://www.goodreads.com/author/quotes/5525291.Chris_Voss

Ware, J. (2019, August 22). The double bind: A leadership challenge for women in business. *Skye Learning.* https://blog.skyelearning.com/the-double-bind-a-leadership-challenge-for -women-in-business

Warwick, J. (n.d.). *Elevating negotiations with emotional intelligence.* ThinkWarwick. https://www.thinkwarwick.com/blog/emotional-intelligence-effective-neg otiation

WebMD Editorial Contributor. (n.d.). *Burnout: Symptoms and signs.* WebMD. https://www.webmd.com/mental-health/burnout-symptoms-signs

Webster, R. (2022, June 9). *Women & negotiation: 5 tips for negotiating better.* LinkedIn. https://www.linkedin.com/pulse/women-negotiation-5-tips-negotiating-b etter-rita-webster-ph-d-?trk=public_post

Westover, J. H. (2023, September 13). *The art of emotional control: Strategies for managing emotions during challenging discussions*. Human Capital I n n o v a t i o n s . https://www.innovativehumancapital.com/post/the-art-of-emotional-control-strategies-for-managing-emotions-during-challenging-discussions

What are some effective ways to understand the other party's perspective during a negotiation? (2023, December 8). LinkedIn. https://www.linkedin.com/advice/1/what-some-effective-ways-understand-other-partys-lkouc

What are some strategies to build rapport and trust before a negotiation? (2023, July 29). LinkedIn. https://www.linkedin.com/advice/0/what-some-strategies-build-rapport-trust

What are the most effective negotiation techniques for building long-term relationships? (2023, December 25). LinkedIn. https://www.linkedin.com/advice/1/what-most-effective-negotiation-techniques-ukyuc

What is stakeholder mapping and how can it help guide negotiations? (2023, March 30). The Maker Group. https://themakergroup.com/what-is-stakeholder-mapping/

Wignall, N. (2022, January 5). *7 ways to discover and clarify your personal values*. Nick Wignall. https://nickwignall.com/know-your-values/

Winkler, C. (2020, June 16). *INSIGHT: Improving virtual negotiation skills in cross-cultural interactions*. Bloomberg Law. https://news.bloomberglaw.com/esg/insight-improving-virtual-negotiation-skills-in-cross-cultural-interactions

Woetzel, L., Madgavkar, A., Ellingrud, K., Labaye, E., Devillard, S., Kutcher, E., Manyika, J., Dobbs, R., & Krishnan, M. (2015). How advancing women's equality can add $12 trillion to global growth. McKinsey & C o m p a n y . https://www.mckinsey.com/featured-insights/employment-and-growth/how-advancing-womens-equality-can-add-12-trillion-to-global-growth#

Wooll, M. (2021, July 26). 13 tips to develop a growth mindset. *BetterUp*. https://www.betterup.com/blog/growth-mindset

Worthy, L. D., Lavigne, T., & Romero, F. (2020, July 27). *Stereotypes and gender roles*. Pressbooks. https://open.maricopa.edu/culturepsychology/chapter/stereotypes-and-gen der-roles/

Zanette, F. (2023, May 25). *The crucial role of preparation in business negotiation*. LinkedIn. https://www.linkedin.com/pulse/crucial-role-preparation-business-negotia tion-federico-zanette

Zilinskas, R. (2023, August 7). *Unlocking success: How a growth mindset propels women forward*. LinkedIn. https://www.linkedin.com/pulse/unlocking-success-how-growth-mindset-propels-women-rosie-zilinskas

Made in the USA
Las Vegas, NV
18 December 2024

14747954R00105